the

        dust

        of

        a

    contact
   that
    is

      everywhere

raymond
    de borja

BUNNY, an imprint of Fonograf Editions
Edited by Ellena Basada, Jeff Alessandrelli & Adie B. Steckel
Portland, OR & New York City, NY

Copyright © 2026 · Raymond de Borja · All rights reserved
Cover and text design by Mike Corrao

First Edition, First Printing
BUNNY09

Published by BUNNY, c/o Fonograf Editions
www.fonografeditions.com/bunny

For information about permission to reuse any material from this book, please contact Fonograf Ed. at info@fonografeditions.com.

Distributed by NYU Press
NYUPress.org

The manufacturer's authorized representative in the EU for product safety is Mare Nostrum Group B.V., Mauritskade 21D, 1091 GC Amsterdam, The Netherlands.
Email: gpsr@mare-nostrum.co.uk.

[c|mp]
Fonograf Editions is a proud member of the Community of Literary Magazines and Presses

ISBN: 978-1-964499-65-9
ISBN (ebook): 978-1-964499-66-6
LCCN: 2025943566

the dust of a contact
that is everywhere

BUNNY

Whether we want it or not, bodies touch on this page, or rather, the page itself is touch (of my hand that is writing, of yours holding this book). This touch is infinitely detoured, deferred – machines, transports, photocopies, eyes, other hands have intervened – but there remains the infinitesimal stubborn grain, the dust of a contact that is everywhere interrupted and everywhere pursued. In the end, your gaze touches the same outlines of characters that mine touches in this moment, and you are reading me, and I am writing for you.

— JEAN-LUC NANCY (trans. Julie Candler Hayes)

I have tried to say
that, although Love is not judgement
analysis too
is a style of affect

— LISA ROBERTSON

CONTENTS

Foreword	xi
They Correspond	3
Selected Days	15
What Happens to Emotions If Collage	35
Lineated Time	39
Pieces	50
Lyric Gesture	62
So Facture Is The Material Fact Of Joy	70
Action, Number, Silence, Work	74
Between The Making Of This Move And This Move	113
The Image As A Knowledge Of Space	117
Aportraiture	123
A House Collaged With Pitch Class Space	131
Works Cited	135
Acknowledgments	139

FOREWORD
PAOLO JAVIER

I write this introduction with deep alarm at how Philippine-U.S. imperialist history continues to bear down on the U.S. American present, and I write in grief over my father's passing this July in Canada, where my mother, my brother and his fiancée, my sister, and her family still live. I grew up under Martial Law in Manila, when censors monitored speech and Ferdinand Marcos Sr.'s regime silenced journalists, artists, writers, and activists through imprisonment, torture, and killing. My family sheltered dissidents in our home before joining the EDSA revolution of 1986 that toppled the U.S.-backed dictatorship. My childhood taught me to see poetry as fragile yet defiant—reminding me that language can wound as easily as it can shelter, that it can serve tyranny and repression but also sustain survival.

This lesson—that poetry could live in tension—followed me into adulthood. But in the world of letters it resurfaced in another form early in my journey as an author: rejection. Twenty years ago, when my first book of poems, *the time at the end of this writing*, appeared in the U.S. and Canada, a Manila newspaper columnist dismissed it. This prominent poet with connections to the Flip writing community in New York mocked my debut's experimentalism while praising the more conventional collection of an older FilAm poet born and raised in the U.S. Dismayed by this conservative gatekeeping, I withdrew from conversations with Philippines-based writers, convinced there was little space for the poetry I most valued.

If Manila's gatekeeping once convinced me there was no room for such work, Raymond de Borja's new book arrives as its counterpoint—a sign that another path has always been possible. This is why *the dust of a contact that is everywhere* feels reparative. Where my poetics were forged in confrontation, de Borja offers another mode: slower, quieter, but no less political in its careful regard. His radicalism lies in close reading akin to devotion, treating the fragment, the collage, and the gesture as ways of building solidarity with writers and artists across time and place. Encountering this work in 2025, and being invited by Fonograf Editions to write alongside it, eases the sting of my earlier rejection and renews my optimism for experimental literature in the Motherland—evidence that it flourishes despite institutional conservatism.

De Borja does not frame his project as conventional criticism but as an ars poetica of kinship. He explains: "Two independent clauses that echo recurring aspects in my work - 1.) A preference for correspondences of things over connections of things, which I practice in collage work, and 2.) Correspondence, as in the correspondence between or among people engaged in various conversations." For him, the fragment is not unfinished but a gesture of relation, a way of keeping company with texts and lives. Lisa Robertson's reminder clarifies this: "Reading shares this necessarily unsanctioned intimacy... I have the strong sense that reading chooses me, as have my friendships." De Borja's writing embodies this same intimacy—less about closure than about keeping voices alive in dialogue.

His influences stretch across continents and disciplines, assembling unexpected correspondences. Philosophers Hannah

Arendt, Walter Benjamin, Maurice Blanchot, Gilles Deleuze and Félix Guattari, Karl Marx, and Benedict Anderson appear beside poets such as Mei-mei Berssenbrugge, Paul Celan, Emily Dickinson, Kurt Schwitters, Barbara Guest, Lyn Hejinian, Susan Howe, and Lisa Robertson. He engages conceptual artists Simon Hantaï and On Kawara, composer Toru Takemitsu, and Filipino contemporaries Marc Gaba and Allan Balisi, while translating Allan Popa's Tagalog poems. Reading such a who's who of 20th century avant garde figures, I can't help but think of José Garcia Villa, whose daring formal inventions made him central to U.S. American modernism, and David Medalla, whose *Signals* gallery and magazine connected experimental artists across London in the 1960s. Perhaps their absence from de Borja's book underscores his aim: not to establish a canon but to assemble a personal archive of resonances. Unlike Villa, whose brilliance carried a prescriptive edge, de Borja cultivates openness, allowing a poetics to emerge through relation rather than decree.

At his most focused, de Borja turns to poets and artists as partners in dialogue, voices that illuminate new pathways. Celan's *Meridian* is one touchstone: "The poem is lonely. It is lonely and underway... The poem wants to reach an Other, it needs this Other, it needs an Over-against. It seeks out, speaks toward it." In his meditation on Allan Popa's *Kasaysayan*, translation becomes encounter, one that steps into history through close attention and utterance: "'Kasaysayan,' which directly translates to history, has in it the word 'say-say' which can mean any of 'value,' 'meaning,' 'statement'... For today, I choose to translate it as utterance."

This attention extends to his reflections on Marc Gaba's Mondrian-inspired paintings, where abstraction resists rigidity and breathes as dialogue with the viewer. Like de Borja, Gaba is both poet and artist; de Borja writes about his friend not from critical distance but in adjacency, where looking, writing, and *pakikisama* converge.

De Borja's prose also absorbs the strategies of writers he esteems, reshaping them into his own style of inquiry. From Lyn Hejinian—my mentor, friend, publisher and north star—he carries forward the new sentence, where thought unfolds by digression and return. In Mei-mei Berssenbrugge, he finds a syntax that slows perception into meditation. With Lisa Robertson, abstraction sharpens into sudden intimacy, clarity edged with eros. De Borja transforms these approaches into an idiom wherein collage, journaling, and translation become a means of companionship across time and place.

This book arrives at a charged political moment. Published in the U.S. by Fonograf Editions—de Borja's first American release—it signals a growing recognition of avantgarde literature from the Philippines, especially following *Glossolalia*, Marlon Hacla's acclaimed 2023 book of surrealist prose from Ugly Duckling Presse. Meanwhile progressive dissent in the United States remains under attack, fueled by MAGA and Project 2025. Reproductive rights and gender-affirming care are curtailed, books vanish from classrooms, universities dismantle programs, artists face censorship for naming the state's violences, and migrants endure scapegoating. Legal immigrants and U.S. citizens of color face intensifying hostility. The Democratic Party fractures as it accepts money from organizations complicit in genocide while performing hollow rebukes against fascism. Such duplicity leaves progressive artists and cultural workers stranded between repression from the right and betrayal from the supposed left. The poetry world clings to prizes and the MFA circuit, while its non-profits fire organizers and remain silent about anti-AAPI hate and the genocide of West Asians in Gaza. Against this backdrop, de Borja's book matters to me all the more: it offers a model of relation and of pause, a way to resist not only the demand for legibility and certainty but also the relentless drive for productivity under late capitalism. In this pause, I seek strength—an interval for rest and reflection that restores my attention to deep reading, and steadies me to respond to our collapsing empire with greater clarity of purpose as a poet.

De Borja also belongs to a broader current of resistance in Pilipino experimental practice. Emmanuel Lacaba carried Rimbaud's dictum that the poet must be "absolutely modern" into the struggle against Martial Law, wielding art as a weapon against tyranny before Marcos's military captured and killed him in 1976. José Garcia Villa recalibrated poetry in English with comma poems and reversed consonance, even as his severe pronouncements closed down dialogue. David Medalla staged participatory avant-garde interventions that turned anti-Marcos propaganda into art. Pacita Abad transformed exile into bold textile canvases confronting dictatorship and displacement. With *But for the Lovers*, Wilfredo Nolledo rebuked Hollywood's WWII Pacific island fantasies, instead inventing a distinctly Pilipino surrealism to depict Manila under the waning shadow of Japanese imperialism. De Borja's poetics belong to this lineage, though it moves differently—anchored in duration: meditative, sustained through dialogue, and marked by vigilance that refuses disappearance.

My father's clarity in the face of authoritarianism sharpens how I read de Borja's work: modest yet unyielding, and a reminder that steady attention itself can be a form of defiance. The son of parents from Ilocos Sur—Marcos Sr's own province—Prim Javier, Jr stood resolute against dictatorship. As treasurer of a U.S. company, Papa refused bribes again and again, including those from Marcos Sr's cronies—choices that placed him at real personal and professional risk. As the husband of a University of the Philippines graduate, he supported my mother's activism and joined her when our family entered the People Power revolution. Papa remained anti-Trump and anti-MAGA. He teaches me that refusal itself can be resistance, a lesson that returns in de Borja's book, where gestures of care endure against empire's demands and the market's lures alike.

With de Borja and Hacla's work now reaching U.S. readers, experimental literature from the Philippines enters a wider conversation, speaking alongside contemporary diasporic Pilipino (North) American avant-garde poets—Jessica Hagedorn, Catalina Cariaga, R. Zamora Linmark, Veronica Corpus, Barbara Jane Reyes, Eileen Tabios, Mg Roberts, Fonograf Editions' own Kimberly Alidio and Charles Valle, Jason Magabo Perez, Sean Labrador, Dennis Somera, Feliz Molina, Celine Shimizu, Shaheen Qureshi, and myself—and visual artists—Josh Kline, Stephanie Syjuco, Mikko Revereza, Christopher Baliwas, Jaret Vadera, Emmy Catedral, and Stephanie Comilang—together sustaining a dialogue that unsettles and dismantles the master's tongue. As my *kababayan* in Manila gather this week at EDSA for the Trillion Peso March against the corruption of Bong Bong Marcos Jr's government and the excesses of oligarchs, the link between Papa's generation and the present moment sharpens. Drawing strength from de Borja's example, I see in his poetics a commitment to resurgence: that in our diffusion, in our cross-border correspondences, in our stubborn departures from the expected, Pilipino experimental literature and art gather force like dust—luminous in spread, eluding enclosure, and persisting to imagine futures empire cannot contain.

PAOLO JAVIER, September 2025, New York City

the
dust
of
a
contact
that
is
everywhere

raymond
de borja

THEY CORRESPOND

"Things do not connect; they correspond," writes Jack Spicer in his letter to the dead Federico Garcia Lorca.

Things do not connect; they correspond—two independent clauses that echo recurring aspects in my work: 1.) A preference for correspondences of things over connections of things, which I practice in collage work, and 2.) Correspondence, as in the correspondence between or among people engaged in various conversations. This pun on correspond is quite salient in *After Lorca*, in its humor and estrangement, as Spicer channels the dead Lorca to write the preface for his book. Here is a part of the preface:

> Frankly I was quite surprised when Mr. Spicer asked me to write an introduction to this volume. My reaction to the manuscript he sent me (and to the series of letters that are now a part of it) was and is fundamentally unsympathetic. It seems to me the waste of a considerable talent on something which is not worth doing. However, I have been removed from all contact with poetry for the last twenty years. The younger generation of poets may view with pleasure Mr. Spicer's execution of what seems to me a difficult and unrewarding task.
>
> It must be clear at the start that these poems are not translations. In even the most literal of them Mr. Spicer seems to derive pleasure in inserting or substituting

one or two words which completely change the mood and often the meaning of the poem as I had written it.

More often he takes one of my poems and adjoins to half of it half of his own, giving rather the effect of an unwilling centaur. (Modesty forbids me to speculate which end of the animal is mine.)

And here is the excerpt from which the epigraph "Things do not connect; they correspond" is taken:

Dear Lorca,
[...]

Things do not connect; they correspond. That is what makes it possible for a poet to translate real objects, to bring them across language as easily as he can bring then across time. That tree you saw in Spain is a tree I could never have seen in California, that lemon has a different smell and a different taste, BUT the answer is this – every place and every time has a real object to correspond with your real object – that lemon may become this lemon, or it may even become this piece of seaweed, or this particular color of gray in this ocean. One does not need to imagine that lemon; one needs to discover it.

Even these letters. They correspond with something (I don't know what) that you have written (perhaps as unapparently as that lemon corresponds to this piece of seaweed) and, in turn, some future poet will write something which corresponds to them. That is how we dead men write to each other.

My keenness to talk about friendship is manifold. In a creative sense, I am grateful to a number of friends for the writing and the visual art work that I do. My work is heavily dependent on prompts and encounters, mostly chance encounters through heard language, conversations, interesting material, and also through willed encounters, for example, in conversation on specific drafts of my work, and friends gifting me with objects they think I can use in collage.

But the more I think of friendships as integral to the creative process, the more interested I become in thinking about how friendship can become a generative potential outside the prevailing rhetoric on friendship (i.e., friendships in relation to social capital, or the perverse realism of social networks and marketing—of "adding/making friends" in relation to the pursuit of profit, or the profitability of corporations). One should note that while friendship, in the realm of thought, is treated in Aristotle's *Nicomachean Ethics* as a fundamental component of practical philosophy, love, particularly the amorous relationship, though perhaps more consequential and affectively complex in lived experience, appears to have been more conceptually elaborated in recent philosophical discourse

Think for instance of entire books on the topic of love. Roland Barthes's abecedarian of the flawed lover in *A Lover's Discourse*, or Alain Badiou's *In Praise of Love* where he masterfully distills the concept of love without reducing its complexity:

> What kind of world does one see when one experiences it from the point of view of two and not one? What is the world like when it is experienced, developed and lived from the point of view of difference and not identity? That is what I believe love to be.

I am interested in how friendship as generative affective links/networks/multiplicities (rather than as rhetorical ruse or social stratagem) is integral to and inscribed in creative work, but at the same time wary that links/networks/multiplicities, even if deemed affective, such as friendship, are also potential sites of hierarchical power structures and false multiplicities. Gilles Deleuze and Felix Guattari refer to this scenario, rather punningly, by invoking the friendship theorem from the field of graph theory:

> [E]ven when one thinks one has reached a multiplicity, it may be a false one – of what we call the radicle type – because its ostensibly nonhierarchical presentation or statement in fact only admits of a totally hierarchical solution. An example is the famous friendship theorem: "If any two given individuals in a society have precisely one mutual friend, then there exists an individual who is the friend of all the others." (Rosenstiehl and Petitot ask who that mutual friend is. Who is "the universal friend in this society of couples: the master, the confessor, the doctor? These ideas are curiously far removed from the initial axioms." Who is this friend of humankind? Is it the philosopher as he appears in classical thought, even if he is an aborted unity that makes itself felt only through its absence or subjectivity, saying all the while, I know nothing, I am nothing?) Thus the authors speak of dictatorship theorems. Such is indeed the principle of roots-trees, or their outcome: the radicle solution, the structure of Power.

Can we trace the affective links of friendship and to see how form, particularly the form of the poem (form taken as the configuration of the materials that is the poem, rather than a prescribed/fixed form) is entangled with it? I am interested in finding out what such entanglements can generate, particularly in the poems of Spicer, Paul Celan, and Mei-mei Berssenbrugge—three rather disparate poets whose treatments of the *you*—that necessary other figure in friendship—allows us to reimagine what connections are possible out of form's and friendship's affective links.

Spicer confounds the boundaries between personal and public address through the form of the letter, maintaining the intimate tone found in letters to lovers and friends, but with an anterior intention of reading these letters to an audience. Most of his epistolary work is found in three books: *After Lorca*, with letters to Lorca interspersed with playful translations of Lorca's own work; *Letters to James Alexander* with letters addressed to a James and to a Jim Alexander (which Spicer did not mean to get published but were posthumously published anyway in *My Vocabulary Did This To Me*, a book of his collected poems); and *Admonitions* with poems and letters dedicated to his poet friends.

In one of his letters to James Alexander, he refers to the expressed annoyance of one of his audience:

Dear James,

It is absolutely clear and absolutely sunny as if neither a cloud nor a moon had ever been invented. I am lying here as if neither a cloud nor a moon had ever been invented. I am lying here on the grass of the University of California, a slave state but one which today seems peculiarly beneficent. I have not had a letter from you in weeks.

I read them all (your letters and mine) to the poets assembled for the occasion last Wednesday. Ebbe was annoyed since he thought letters should remain letters (unless they were essays) and poems poems (a black butterfly just flew past my leg) and that the universe of the personal and the impersonal should be kept in order. George Stanley thought that I was robbing Jim to pay James. They sounded beautiful all of them.

In Spicer's letter, we see the poet playfully map a topology of affective links—from poet to addressee, letter sender to receiver, performer to audience—eliciting a range of responses spanning from disinterest, wonder, and frustration. In one of his letters to Lorca, Spicer admits to the frustration he feels from not having an audience to his poems, "I may not be a better poet when I am in love, but I am a far less frustrated one. My poems have an audience [...] All this to explain why I dedicate each of our poems to someone," Spicer writes.

Although Spicer's playful tracings hint at and point to potential topologies of friendship by complicating boundaries of personal and public space, I want to turn to Paul Celan to look at an affirmative and more nuanced topology of the necessity of friendship as a condition of the poem—a topology where friendship is inscribed in, and is integral to the poem. Here is an oft-cited passage from his *Meridian* speech which I present in three versions: first in the John Felstiner translation, then in the Rosmarie Waldrop translation and lastly the original German text:

> The poem is lonely. It is lonely and underway. Whoever writes one stays mated with it. But in just this way

doesn't the poem stand, right here, in an encounter – in the mystery of an encounter?

The poem wants to reach an Other, it needs this Other, it needs an Over-against. It seeks out, speaks toward it.
    (trans. John Felstiner)

The poem is lonely and en route. It's author stays with it. Does this very fact not place the poem already here, at its inception, in the encounter, in the mystery of encounter?

The poem intends another, needs this other, needs an opposite. It goes towards it. It bespeaks it.
    (trans. Rosmarie Waldrop)

Das Gedicht ist einsam. Es ist einsam und unterwegs. Wer es schreibt, bleibt ihm mitgebeben. Aber steht das Gedicht nicht gerade dadurch, also schon hier, in der Begegnung – im Geheimnis der begegnung?

Das Gedicht will zu einem Andern, es braucht dieses Andere, es braucht ein Gegenbür. Es sacht es auf, es spricht sich ihm zu.

Needless to say it is impossible, and in the excerpts presented above, unnecessary to talk about a definitive translation of Celan's texts (though, in general, some translations are more adept than others). A more worthwhile task might be to regard each translation as a valid reading, and to examine the meaningful variations that arise from these interpretive differences. For instance, in the last two sentences of the excerpted passages we can note the following:

1. The play on "an-Other"—"einem" being the German equivalent of the English article "A" and "Andern" the German word for "other," but also for "changing" or "altering." This play compounds the tracings if one were to look at the topology formed by other/another in terms of difference and similarity, and inclusion and exclusion.
2. "Gegen" is the German equivalent of the preposition meaning "towards," but also of "against" and "around." "Uber" is the German for "over" (hence the translation "Over- against"), but "Gegenuber" taken as a word translates to English as the word "opposite." This compounds the tracings of the sentence in terms of directionality.
3. "Will zu" translated by Felstiner as "wants to reach" (with a tone of desire) but which Waldrop translates to intends (closer to creation, as in "designing another").

But the more interesting variation happens in the translation of the phrase "Wer es schreibt" which directly translates to English as "who writes," but which Felstiner chooses to translate to "whoever writes," and Waldrop translates to "author" (in German note that author typically translates to Autor or Versfasser).

The precise impersonality of "who writes" rather than the generic, seemingly random "whoever writes" or the hierarchical, and also limiting, status of the "author" allows us to read in Paul Celan a possible map of friendship (from an indefinite "one who writes" linked to/intending/going to others, an Other, many others). Is this not analogous to the "Who?" that Maurice Blanchot in his essay on friendship—written on the occasion of his friend, George Bataille's death—speaks of when he says:

> I also know that in his books, George Bataille seems to speak of himself with a freedom without restraint that should free us from all discretion – but that does not give us the right to put ourselves in his place, nor does it give us the power to speak in his absence. And is it certain that he speaks of himself? The "I" whose presence his search seems still to make manifest when it expresses itself, toward whom does it direct us?
> [...]
>
> "Who was the subject of this experience?" this question is perhaps already an answer if, even to him who led it, the experience asserted itself in this interrogative form, by substituting the openness of a "Who?" without answer for the closed and singular "I."

So one can take the poem, as Celan describes it in the Meridian speech, as analogous to the form of the letter but written by an indefinite (multiple?) "Who?" to another, towards others.

———

I want to turn now to Mei-mei Berssenbrugge to look at explorations of the intensities present in the affective links of friendship. If through Spicer we are able to view friendship as a social creative space, and in Celan as intrinsic to the poem, I want to ask what intensities are present in the affective links of friendship. In attempting to map the affective links of friendship as inscribed in and as a necessary condition for poems, apart from mapping the geometries linking "Who?" to "Others", one must also ask – how is it possible to have an affective but non-sentimental attitude towards persons in a friendship? Berssenbrugge offers the possibility of such space in "Kisses from the Moon":

> I'm so pleased to be friends with Maryanne, though I don't understand how she has time for me, with her many friends.
> The event of friendship opens, making afterward a field of possibility from which to begin, tenderness pre-existing.
> At my party, how does friendship sometimes light her being there, sometimes possibility itself?
> Let the sensation, "I listen to her," dissolve in my head; there's no self.
> What's called hearer is hearing.
>
> An exemplary listener is determined, who pre-exists my wish to be heard.
> She loses this presumed identity through singular beauty, one dividing the other.
> Perhaps, "Can you hear me in the night?" exaggerates friendship.
> Its featherweight vulnerability offers no counter-weight for care through that night?

In Berssenbrugge, this non-sentimental affective space is enacted through an exercise in attention. Formally, through the long sentence-line where attention is held, released, and reined in again through the minimal music in an alternating conjunctive and disjunctive space of discourse. But also atmospherically, where while intimacy is evident—enacted here through the dissolution of self in pure perception ("hearer is hearing")—it is not used to produce mere narrative effects, but rather to intensify the becoming of affective relations. An intensity of relation, one that in Berssenbrugge reaches its most vivid articulation in a speculative and therefore aspirational register (we imagine what we aspire to), becomes a phenomenologically felt reality: "What if I write to you and you feel me?"

And so a potential, expansive topology of friendship begins to take shape, traced through Spicer's play on the private and the public, Berssenbrugge's speculatively and intimately linked *I* and *you*, Celan's precisely impersonal *who*, and the unknowability inherent in Blanchot's *friend*. Blanchot allows us to expand this topology further:

> Friendship this relation without dependence, without episode, yet into which all of the simplicity of life enters, passes by way of the recognition of the common strangeness that does not allow us to speak of our friends but only to speak to them, not to make them a topic of conversations (or essays), but the movement of understanding in which, speaking to us, they reserve, even on the most familiar terms, an infinite distance, the fundamental separation on the basis of which what separates becomes relation.

In Blanchot, friendship is relational yet *without dependence; without episode,* it resists being neatly enclosed within narrative, yet remains the space where our lives can meet in a shared, *common strangeness.* Relations are not configured toward specific ends but toward *inhabiting a movement of understanding.* It is a space where even the closest and most familiar gain *infinite,* inexhaustible *distance.* Is this not, in another sense, a space in which we could live a creative life?

SELECTED DAYS

DECEMBER 27

Today I attempt something of a journal, a *Tagebuch*, a sleep diary. I want to have something I can work with and mark with days.

I am thinking about music and why "to understand music" does not make sense in the same way that "to understand instructions," or "to understand a novel" does. In thinking about what it means "to understand music," I find the term abstract quite useful; not abstract when used pejoratively to describe incomprehensible mishmash, or to refer to some general outline of an idea, but abstract meaning non-referential: where meaning emerges mainly from other than reference – for example, from the relationship among notes, rhythm, scale, color.

Some notes on Gordon Matta-Clark and Richard Serra: while both works allow for a geometric experience of space, Serra works with pure/asocial forms—lines, planes, curves; while one can say of Matta-Clark that he works with social forms—lines, planes, curves abstracted, for example, from a condemned building.

From an engineering perspective, these asocial forms are harder to produce.

> white overheard
> song overhead
> whence, when, when sung

R.d.B.

One begins to understand composition. I saw again a picture of what a few days ago I thought was a plastic bag floating in the afternoon wind, casting its shadow on the asphalt ground.

Looking at it again, this time closely, I see that it is a window. The plastic bag is not a plastic bag at all, but a flimsy curtain. How had this detail so easily escaped me?

I am reminded of Andrew Wyeth's curtain in *Wind from the Sea*. The beautiful sense of dislocation affected by the transparent curtain in mid-flap, in the foreground, carrying with it the slightly fuzzed landscape of the background.

This experience of being in a house. I am thankful for windows.

FEBRUARY 26

To invent is to present the new as something useful. Thinking in this light, then gleaning from this thinking that utility is the domain of prose and not of poetry, then the new in poetry is not an invention. Jack Spicer takes this further when to a dead Federico Garcia Lorca, he writes, "Prose invents—poetry discloses." Poetry as disclosure—was Spicer hinting at the Heideggerean *aletheia*? That is, truth conceived as the revelation of being rather than adherence to objective reality, with poetry enacting the very process of concealment and unconcealment through which truth emerges.

Yet, we must be wary, too, of disclosure. While one has to move from mere appearances to access being, this access, as *aletheia*, Hannah Arendt observes, is still conceivable as a form of appearance. Always then, we merely approach and approach the metaphysical closure.

> To not do anything
> but approach
> thing music
> the rough outline
> the grass strains toward
> the simple present

I read Jack Spicer's letters again, and again, and am fascinated by their formal beauty—the letters in *After Lorca*, which become a vehicle for all the beautiful rhetoric that Spicer wants rid of his poems; his *Letters to James Alexander*, where a *you* is made manifest through the sheer intimacy and specificity of address.

R.d.B.

In Badiou, the new is something that the existing language cannot yet describe. Taking from Heiddeger, he defines the truth as "something new": as something ushered in through a rupture in the logic of appearance, a rupture which he calls an *event*, recognizing that this "naming of an *event* or of the *evental* presence is itself poetic."

Dear Jean,

I am writing to you because this pastoral needs another person. We have leaves already and the guests have left. When will you pick up the PVC, the trees, our invention? This is our invention, yet men die miserably, every day, for lack of what is not found there.

MAY 14.

There are two easy ways out when dealing with questions on the authenticity of the experience of art: the romantic—the cloying notion of art as expression of the self and so, as a given, capable of speaking to other selves; and the sociologic – art as nothing more than a product of social relations. Yet, neither paradigm seems to me generative (with generative thought being, in my practice, a necessary condition for the production and thinking through of art). It is only through a disregard of the many discourses on the self that we can return to the romantic (is it hope that drives us to want such a return?); and the sociologic, more a realm of the quantifiable than of thought, cannot offer a space that makes a hopeful thinking for and of *authenticity* and of *art* possible.

Perhaps Jean-Luc Nancy, through his book *Listening*, offers not a way out but a clearing of sorts, which is capable of making generative again the discussions on the authenticity of the experience of art.

Nancy—and here perhaps addressing Bela Bartok's statement that "those who do not know how to read or play music cannot really listen to it"—asks, "If someone listens to music without knowing anything about it – as we say of those who have no knowledge of musicology [...], is it possible that he is actually listening to it, rather than being reduced to hearing it?"

While recognizing that "technical apprehension and sensory apprehension" do "strengthen" and "sharpen" each other, in *Listening*, Nancy resituates music as that which makes possible a sonorous place where the art object and the perceiver are no longer held through a simple subject-object relationship. The sonorous place is where a subject, listening, is referred back to itself not as object, but as a listening subject.

A note outside notational space is time.

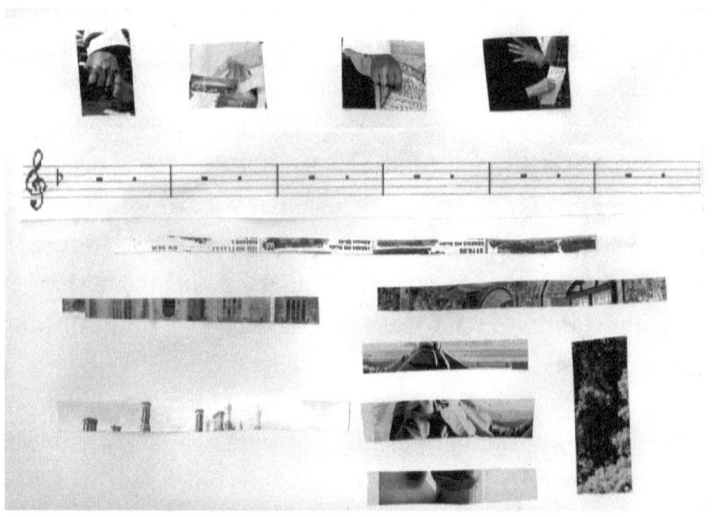

Image courtesy of the author, May 2012.

1. Notes on two possible sutures for image and sound: 1. Toru Takemitsu asking the director Masahiro Shinoda to cut scenes that do not work well with his musical score. Shinoda to Takemitsu: "But when I heard that Turkish flute music at the mix, I was amazed. You were right, this is how the film should end"

2. John Zorn expressing his fascination for Carl Stalling's scores for 30s/40s Bugs Bunny cartoons: "He (referring to Stalling) was dealing with an image and trying to sync music with the image. Take the image away and you're dealing with something that doesn't make musical sense"

The sound of a yellow line
The string section accompanies the sand
Through a megaphone his musings
Wind wound

Image courtesy of the author, May 2012.

MAY 27.

In the opening scene of The Face of Another (directed by Hiroshi Teshigahara, music by Toru Takemitsu), we are faced by a crowd; the music is waltz. What binds the music to the image is not atmosphere but the movement of a crowd. The scene is a dance.

Still from The Face of Another, 1966, dir. Hiroshi Teshigahara.

———

"[F]aced with the voice, words structurally fail," Mladen Dolar writes in A Voice and Nothing More. The project then is not description; instead, it is the enabling of experience. In a movement towards sound, images become lines, literally.

t.d.o.a.c.t.i.e.

Image courtesy of the author, May 2012.

R.d.B.

JUNE 10.

More than its attention to cadence, breath, and sound, and how these are notated in a poem via lineation, the spirit of projective verse, and I take spirit to differentiate between a formal fad and an enduring poetic value, is its foregrounding of a poem as a *field* of perception via an attention to the poem's units of composition. Today, rereading Stéphane Mallarmé, in the essay *Limited Action*, describe the poem as being "gifted only with a feeble power," and advise the poet to "perjure [his] verse," I turn to the spirit of projective verse as that which gives the contemporary lyric poem its potency—as a possible space not only for the critique of spectacular modes of perception, but also for the creation of alternatives to the spectacular mode.

Away from the spectacle, in a movement towards sound, the aural imagination of place:

> Fray was the name where we came
> to next. Might've been a place,
> might not've been a place but
> we were there, came to it
>   sooner
> than we could see... Come to
> so soon, it was a name we stuck
> pins in hoping we'd stay. Stray
> was all we ended up with. Spar
> was another name we heard
>   it
> went by... Rasp we also heard it
>   was

called...   Came to it sooner
than we could see but soon enough
saw we were there. Some who'd
come before us called it Bray...
Sound's own principality it was,
a pocket of air flexed mouthlike,
meaning's mime and regret, a squib of
something said, so intent it
seemed.

(from "Song of the Andomboulou: 50" by Nathaniel Mackey)

In a movement towards sound, the term *abstract* is useful—where meaning is produced from other than reference. In the sonorous place (*sound's principality*), meaning is consistently deferred - always towards a suggestion of meaning (*meaning's mime*), yet never fully crystallizing (*meaning's regret*). Fray - stray -spar - rasp- bray - words functioning outside their lexical definition, and standing in for *place*, where sound is so persistent, *so intent it/ seemed*.

In Section 15 of "The Work of Art in the Age of Mechanical Reproduction," Walter Benjamin, on the phenomenology of buildings, writes: "Buildings are appropriated in a twofold manner: by use and by perception—or rather, by touch and sight"; noting that because buildings (architecture) are spatial constructs, purely optical means i.e. "attentive concentration" will not suffice to undertake their appropriation. Benjamin notes as well how we can take the appropriation of buildings as instructive of the kind of attention required to tackle the problematic of disinterested modes of perception: "The tasks which face the human apparatus of perception at the turning points of history cannot be solved by optical means, that is, by contemplation, alone. They are mastered gradually by habit, under the guidance of tactile appropriation."

———

Staying in the house, what I see is not a building but a room with *Yellow Tulips* by Charles Rennie Mackintosh in 1922:

This room, like many other rooms, is comprised of planes. One creased plane is the curtain. The plane-curtain is creased by rough swaths of white paint on black. Yellow grows from the paint can as tulips. The tulips, each takes a different direction, each to its own source of light.

NOVEMBER 18.

Today I am thinking of a long beautiful line, and I am thinking an affect can distribute attention in the same way that the city architecture does not hold my attention but lays it on several glass windows with the gridded sky. Longing for a horizon line, where, glint-like, fishing boats bob up and down to bird calls, the shifting surface of attention. In what ways do we resemble architecture but are not it—to be an entire window? Here the category 'beautiful things' can be used for things that shift the direction of a line towards a newfound attentiveness, which for instance is the unfamiliar familiar door knob sheen tree light afternoon. So when someone says, today is a beautiful day, we can build her a story where everything goes her way, or we can build her a morning where she wakes up to things that in some mornings may have caught our attention: sound frame, thing music, night timbre.

———

Sound Prop #1: Sound Frame

> except she finds it difficult to see
>
> which meant to put together
>
> ings are images. Portmanteau
>
> ries of diagonals frame wobbles
>
> (sic) sounds cut he frame here

Image courtesy of the author.

She leans at a big window overlooking Rue Rousseau. A tiny cafe spills out onto the street, runs past droves of arriving concert- goers, and heads for the theater. Music continues. The clock hands its share. Signs everywhere of, and the sound slides. They are making an appointment. So we walk in a garden of trumpets, and smoke, and knocks on doors, to the sound of the market before the market, static leaves. We are, our faces, found by footsteps.

———

Sound Prop #2: Thing Music

> to not do
> anything but
> approach thing
> music the rough
> outline the grass
> strains toward
> the simple present

———

The music is her temperament, writing letters as Susan.

———

Sound Prop #3: Night Timbre

DECEMBER 9.

Alain Badiou re-presents the Platonic banishment of the poem and offers a reversal. In Plato, the poem is differentiated from the matheme through the dialectic of the sensible and the intelligible. The poem being "a form of thought that is inseparable from the sensible," while mathematics is a "thought [that is] immediately written as thought;" hence, "poetry [as] thought that is not a thought, a thought that is not even thinkable."

Yet the modern poem has an undeniably "intelligible vocation." Recognizing that the poem's presentation of the sensible does not necessarily place it in opposition to the intelligible/thought, Badiou, in outlining the disjunction of the poem from the matheme, turns away from the Platonic dialectic and moves towards the poem's and the matheme's Real—the real of the matheme being the consistency of language (the necessity of consistency for mathematics to operate as mathematics), the real of the poem being the power of language (the impossibility of the meta-poem, the powerlessness of the poem to name its power).

As such, in Badiou, both poem and matheme become necessary conditions for the thinking of being, event and truth—the essentially poetic activity of the naming of an event which in turn ushers in truth, and the mathematically rigorous fidelity (a deductive consistency) to this truth. Thinking of Mallarmé's *A Throw of Dice*, Badiou writes: "The poem [...] subordinates sensible desire to the aleatory advent of the Idea. The poem is a duty of thought."

In *The End of the Poem*, Giorgio Agamben writes of an "essential disjunction" which inheres in the versed lyric poem, between the "semiotic event" (sound/repetition of a sound) and the "semantic event" (sense). Perhaps, it is in this essential space of non-coincidence where the "aleatory advent of the Idea" can occur in the lyric poem:

> Like the ghost of a woman from ruin
> to doors with one pair of shoes
>
> in a drenching rain
> or when a spirit in bird-form hits the glass
>
> I waved farewell by the lash
> of my eyes, to say goodbye
>
> to romance --once--and much time passed
>
> (from "Lines out to Silence," Fanny Howe)

In Agamben, this disjunction, which makes a verse *a verse*, poses a paradoxical identity crisis for the poem when the poem ends: when sense (normally through the end-stopped line) finally coincides with sound. Of the ending of the poem, Agamben quotes Dante on the canzone: "The ending of the last verses are most beautiful if they fall into silence together with the rhymes."

But it is possible to frame this falling into silence as a non-knowing, or as a non-closure (thinking of Keat's negative capability, or of Hejinian's rejection of closure) where sound ends but does not necessarily give in to an understanding of what the poem means, but instead ends with an invitation to re-enter and experience again the poem's movement which is also the poem's meaning.

The ruin-rain glass-lash where much time passed.

―――

To Philip Glass
The first beams of the sun are evidently copies
Time among the engines and ambient
chatter. Time sounds like this day: again
and again, her footsteps with the flowers, morning drawn out
in the space of a street, again and again
at the speed of ambient chatter.
And Glass-like fills the ear with buckets
and buckets of flowers.
Sun and engines, and her
till the morning is drawn out fully
at the speed of ambient flowers

―――

A day is composed of several lines. One composes a day through several lines. Several lines compose a day. The last lines of a daybook fall into a day. A note falls in time

Sound Prop #4: Time

♩

R.d.B.

DECEMBER 26.

A day does not come together except under the mark of a day. A year is not an accumulation of days, but a view of the several lines opened up by several days. In essaying the days through notes on the arts, I reach the fact of non-coherence—there are several days. Composition here, then, is a selection of days, which could also mean that composition constitutes an ethics; we choose the days.

In a state of the arts, where we are presented with several binary opposites, it is important to choose a multitude, a choice that in no way means to choose all. Simone Weil says of the "relative" that it is "not the opposite of the absolute; it is derived from [the absolute] through a relationship which is not commutative." Through Weil, it is possible to think of the absolute not as a law, but as an infinite set of potentialities, and to think of the relative, not as a never-ending series of differentiation where everyone is right, but as an ethical potential, a choice from an infinite set of possibles.

———

from *A Notebook for Film Music*

We enter a scene as a layer of sound enters the small windowless room as time. Breath slips out of the oboe and is heard as breath while the violin waits. What slips in we call music. The room is made of layers of time shut from the outside time telling us the music itself is time and is a wall. We revise enter. We enter the scene which is sound contingent upon another sound and so on.

His idea of time is regular but he feels it in the room as layers. Trying to locate the sounds, he finds them separable and shifting though the room is always itself and has white walls. A page turns with the piano, and a gasp, before the oboe sustains an expanding note in the room, filling up time.

He goes outside the room from time into the wind and sand. The wind and sand are sounds but are not time. The wind shifts the sand as a sharply drawn bow against the strings of the violin. Heat is nowhere to be heard so it is there as silence. He can still hear the room in the shifting wind, but not as memory, but as one hears a real present thing, a source-less after-presence, as one sees the sun in the sand after attempting to look at it in the sky.

———

What then is a day? In journal writing, a day is a multiplicity. Gertrude Stein: "Everything is the same except composition and time, composition and the time of the composition and the time in the composition." In a journal, the time of composition and the time in the composition are both days; taking from Stein, these are separate days. What binds the days together are their movements – each a heterogeneous directionality marked by its movement towards another day. We can choose a day to be our composition as we are composed by days, and we can choose this relationship to be non-commutative. "We [can] sing to be ourselves tomorrow"—borrowing from Lyn Hejinian. If we say of music that it eludes the present in both its progression and resounding, then we can say of the present that it is located at the end of the music. A long, glaring present in the desert heat. Composition is the experience of duration. An aural imagination of On Kawara's date paintings, and Roman Opalka's number paintings suggests an imagined movement towards a present. We can say of both, that they were looking for days. We can say of a composition, that it fills the present as it defers it. We can say that a journal when offered to a reader must end in we.

(Dec 2011 – Dec 2012)

WHAT HAPPENS TO EMOTIONS IF COLLAGE

Today is not July 26, 1972 but we are with it
presently—where "Time is thin around the cause
and dense around the effect," where On Kawara quotes
the Russian astrophysicist Nikolai Kozyrev,
when today is Dec. 28, 2011 and we forget present, and past,
and persist only in July 26, 1972.

This occurs on Dec 28, 2011.
This occurs in July 26, 1972.

This in January—

A period of intense and demanding work begins with the letter J in an elongated, white, Gill Sans. If a painting is not finished by the end of the day, he destroys it.

Or a period of intense and demanding work begins, and is interrupted by oneself: "Now I have arrived at a brilliant means of articulation in the field of reproducing nature," Kurt Schwitters writes to Helma Schwitters. "You see, it is another that paints—I am not he."

On Oct 8, 1983, while Schwitters is living as a refugee in London, the first Merzbau is destroyed by a bomb, in an air raid over Hannover, Germany.

R.d.B.

On Dec 16, 1951, a second Merzbau, constructed from scratch, in Lysaker, Oslo, is completely consumed by fire.

While Schwitters does not refer to the cottage in Hjertoya as a Merzbau, it too is destroyed from neglect and by extreme weather conditions.

On Kawara destroys a painting of Nov.30.197

On Kawara destroys a painting of 30 Nov 198

In August of 1947, Kurt Schwitters begins work on a third Merzbau, which is left unfinished, and significantly damaged after his death.

"It was my prayer for the victorious end to the war, for once more peace emerged victorious again," Kurt writes to Helma.

Dear Jean,

In attempting to erase an object's original reference, its *eigengift*, Kurt Schwitters breaks things that are not broken, and fixes things that are, then glues and nails them together, and are Merz.

What happens to emotions if collage propels our chance meeting? Dear, Darling, We find us echoed in a letter.

t.d.o.a.c.t.i.e.

Dear Jean,

I write to you and illegibly in this pastoral are two persons.

Where we find a limit in the thinking of space-time as a reality, or as an abstraction.

On July 4, 1968, On Kawara sees Jovita Perez Franco, Luis Nishizawa, Adela Miazga;

Magdalena Hashimoto, Luis Urias, Alfred Frederic Wyttenbach, also on July 4, 1968.

Dear Jean,

I write to you and illegibly, we are two pastorals in this person. Persons are refrains.

We know this from On Kawara's "I Met" where he lists, every day, the names of people he meets from 1968 to 1979.

In a letter to Josef Albers, Helma Schwitters writes: "I do not know whether you know we are no longer allowed to exhibit abstract things here; nor can we show them to anyone, for you don't know if your closest friend will betray you or not."

In "I Met," the presence of Hiroko Hiraoko appears on many days. Helma visits Kurt in Oslo, on June 2, 1939, and this is the last time they meet.

After years of demanding work building the Cathedral of Erotic Misery, Schwitters turns to his friends. "The Big E is finished. All that remains are details in a few places and for that I need material and this is why I am turning to you."

In Kawara, a coherent, narrative, unfolding of a life is made legible through the friends he writes to or meets. A friend receives a postcard that says "I got up " or "I am still alive"

Such that one feels a limit in representations of space-time when thinking of Schwitters and Kawara, and one finds this limit in another person.

In Hiroko Hiraoka and Helma Schwitters.

What is missing in Wilhelm Redemann's photographs of a Merzbau, which is the basis for the reconstructions by Peter Bisseger, is conversation among friends.

In some paradoxes, the limit is when friendship happens. Such that friendship is radiating space.

LINEATED TIME
(SOME THOUGHTS ON THE LINE IN POETRY)

Two problems, first of beginning, then of cohering, beset me as I contended with the topic of this essay. Beginning and cohering are obviously elementary features of typical expository forms; but problematic, more so, for a topic that one finds fundamental and elusive. Elusive because it is fundamental in one's own practice of reading and writing.

Here are three thoughts to possibly begin with:

First, the poem is a field of perception with a focus on semiotic-semantic (prosodic-semantic) slippages as opposed to an anthrocentric view that designates the poet's breath as central to the poem.

Second, the potency of the poem is a space for resisting disinterested modes of perception through a reading of the formal choices made in the poem.

Third, ekphrasis thinks about attention and modes of attention instead of descriptions of, or narrative speculations on, the painterly subject matter.

I take the *line* in poetry, the poetic line, as a potential place of convergence, a *topos* for elaborating these three fields of concerns. In the third thesis of his fascinatingly rigorous polemic, titled *Fifteen Theses on Contemporary Art*, Badiou writes of an art "that is the process of a truth," a truth "that is always the truth of the sensible or sensual, the sensible as sensible," and further writes of this artistic truth as neither "a copy of the sensible world nor a static sensible expression."

An artistic truth, then, "is a new proposition about a new definition of what is our sensible relation to the world." The minor project of this essay is of the poetic line and the possibilities offered by the line in terms of renewing our sensible relation to the world.

———

constant change figures

constant change figures
the time we sense
passing on its effect
surpassing things we've known before
since memory
of many things is called experience
but what of what
we call nature's picture
surpassing things we call since memory
we call nature's picture
surpassing things we've known before
constant change figures
experience
passing on its effect
but what of what
constant change figures
since memory
of many things is called
the time we sense
called nature's picture

> but what of what
> in the time we sense
> surpassing things we've known before
> passing on its effect
> is experience

(from *The Book of a Thousand Eyes* by Lyn Hejinian)

One possible way of reading the Hejinian poem is to think of it as a poetic demonstration of the Hegelian critique of the Kantian perception of experience. Kant, by relegating all knowledge to the transcendental consciousness, the *"I think"* (as separate from the *"I am"*), disallows experience from ever becoming knowledge. Hegel, on the other hand, designates experience as the very essence of the subject. Agamben elucidates the point further by quoting from Hegel's *Phenomenology of Spirit*: "The dialectic movement which consciousness exercises on itself, and which affects both its knowledge and its object is precisely what is called experience [Erfahrung]."

Keeping to this reductive reading, we can go on and conclude that what the poem "constant change figure" merely does is poeticize the Hegelian concept of experience through an unfolding and enmeshed relationship between change, time, experience, memory and "nature's picture." But what keeps *constant change figures* from being a mere container of poeticized thought is its wonderful wielding of the line.

"Wonder" from the Old English "wundrian" meaning *to be astonished*. Hejinian's lines transform language itself into experience. Through the minimal shifts in meaning resulting from the changing positions of repeating lines, one experiences experience—as memory, as déjà vu, as present memory. The sameness of the lines is analogous to our very experience of chronology: that of one durational moment after another. Taken in relation to the book where "constant change figures" belongs, *The Book of A Thousand Eyes*, Hejinian's homage to *One Thousand and One Nights*, and taking "constant change figures" as representative of one night, one can read the said night as an attempt at deferring the ending by extending duration, and extending presentness itself.

A line then which along with and in relation to other prosodic and syntactic units of composition configures, apart from describes, our temporal relation to a spatio-temporal and peopled world.

A CARAFE, THAT IS A BLIND GLASS.
A kind in glass and a cousin, a spectacle and nothing strange a single hurt color and an arrangement in a system to pointing. All this and not ordinary, not unordered in not resembling. The difference is spreading.
 (from *Tender Buttons* by Gertrude Stein)

On one end of the spectrum, the problem with ekphrasis that is content with describing, or narrativizing the figures in its subject matter, is that more often than not the resulting description, or story, is already implicit in the artwork itself. Interesting stories may result, but the far more wonderful encounter with new ways of dealing with visuality is ignored. On the other end of the spectrum, ekphrasis, with the intent of duplicating visual modes of perception *in* language fails when the transference verges on the literal or the analogical.

Gertrude Stein's poem is a counterexample to either ends of the spectrum, and also highlights that while the openness of Steinian texts has generated a variety of wonderful readings, those that focus on her poems as a sort of "verbal cubism" somehow diminishes the power of Steinian modes of description by reading them as a replication of visual modes of perception into linguistic modes of representation. (Needless to say, "verbal cubism" has already achieved the status of a canned response to Steinian texts, almost already cited along with her relationship with Picasso.) The attempt at simultaneous, multiple perspectives which cubism deftly executes in the visual space is an *a priori* failed attempt in language because one pursues spatial logic in language's primarily temporal domain.

I turn to the lines of Barbara Guest, in particular the poem "Nebraska," for examples of lines that exhibit an astute awareness of the limitations of linguistically working with visual modes, yet at the same time are able to *create something* out of such limitations. Although borrowing from painterly modes of impressionistic perception, one must not read here an attempt at copying visual reality. One must read neither a supplementary Nebraska (enhancing representations of an actual one) nor a complementary Nebraska (forming an image of an "essential" Nebraska). One can read an invented, a potential Nebraska, even, poised at the sensible space where the actual and virtual meet.

Nebraska

Climate succumbing continuously as water gathered
into foam or Nebraska elevated by ships
withholds what is glorious in its climb like
a waiter balancing a waterglass while the tray

R.d.B.

slips that was necklace in the arch of bridge
now the island settles linear its paragraph of tree
vibrates the natural cymbal with its other tongue
strikes an attitude we have drawn there on the limb
when icicle against the sail will darken the wind
eftsooning it and the ways lap with spices as
buoyancy once the galloping area where grain
is rinsed and care requires we choose our walk

And the swift nodding becomes delicate
smoke is also a flow the pastoral calm where
each leaf has a shadow fortuitous as word
with its pine and cone its seedling a curl
like smoke when the ashy retrograding slopes
at the station up or down and musically
a notation as when smoke enters sky

The swift nodding becomes delicate
'lifelike' is pastoral an ambrosia where calm
produces a leaf with a shadow fortuitous as word
with its pine and cone its seedling we saw
yesterday with the natural flow in our hand
thought of as sunlight and wisely found rocks
sand that were orisons there a city in
our minds we called silence and bird droppings
where the staircase ended that was only roof

Hallucinated as Nebraska the swift blue
appears formerly hid when approached now it
chides with a tone the prow striking a grim
atmosphere appealing and intimate as if a verse
were to water somewhere and hues emerge

and distance erased a swan concluding bridge
the sky with her neck possibly brightening
the machinery as a leaf arches through its yellow
syllables to Nebraska's throat

(from *Forces of Imagination* by Barbara Guest)

The lines in "Nebraska" push language to its syntactical limit while still keeping to the basic order of reading in English—the reading eye's movement from the left to right, up to down (this as opposed to, say, examples from visual poetry which makes one question or even abandon typical orders of reading). By moving from left to right, then up to down, by keeping with the sequential expectations of normative syntax but at the same time relying more on non-syntactical elements of language for its meaning-making, "Nebraska" complicates our experience of space by looking at possibilities of experiencing space when space is stretched in a temporal domain. A domain where *eftsooning* is a verb, and a swan from the imagined Nebraska shares its neck with the bridge, the sky, and Nebraska itself, allowing Nebraska to sing a yellow syllable from its throat.

Agamben, reading the linguist Gustave Guillaume, notes that our typical representation of time as an infinite line, segmented according to past-present-future. This is an inadequate time-image because it is too perfect: "It shows us a time already constructed, but it does not show time in the act of constructing itself in the thought." As a solution to this, Guillaume defines an operational time, the time it takes the mind to realize the time image. A fuller representation of time then is no longer a simple linear representation but a contiguous representation consisting of:

1.) a representation of chronological time (chronologic time being the time where we are, but also which Agamben notes is where we are powerless spectators of ourselves), and

2.) an operational time. This fuller, contiguous representation is what Guillaume refers to as a chronogenetic time, "a time which includes its own genesis," that shows how time temporalizes itself.

Earlier in the same essay, Agamben acknowledges that our simplistic "spatial representation of time—the point, the line, the segment, the circle, etc.—is responsible for a falsification that makes our time experience unthinkable."

Perhaps we can turn to the poetic line as a means to make manifest, if not to represent, the incongruencies of our thinking of time with our experience of it. In Hejinian's "constant change figures," where we are poised at the meaning making that happens as the syntactical units of word and phrase brush up against the line and the repetition of the same lines; and in Guest's "Nebraska" where the visual-representational mode finds itself in a syntactic-temporal domain. But what is missing thus far from these examples is the person.

In both examples, the person is outside the motion of these lines. Though there is a we in both Hejinian and Guest's poems, these are not actively feeling persons but rather figures, exempt from the anxieties, frustrations, wonder, the various affective states generated as a person experiences a time that is thinkable but non-representable and vice versa.

I turn to Berssenbrugge long lines as experiencing these complex affective states:

1

The sky and movement of clouds figure in the issue of
>the frame of the spring, just as
a freeze fifty years ago figures in the tension of
>vegetation regarding its boundaries, now.
Touching the body, its waste and involuntary
>movements figure in tensions regarding her frame,
relating planets to moon in a strip above the spring.
>She talks of contained space,
as if frame were sometime made in the body, that
>might be stepped on, not tripped over, grass,
slippage between her family existence and establishing
>imprecise area. She walks by.
The spring reflects her looking and space around her.
>Then space is rejected for internal
shifts of weight and balance, highly charged as sky
>next to the left side of his face.
His body is a response I get from somewhere else, as if
>things began telling my thoughts,
rocks, red crows, while she stays on the periphery of
>what I see and hear.
Everything's in the field to designate and stabilize,
>plants evenly spaced by water.
A pellet of sand rolls down, leaving a trail behind. In-
>depth seriality takes time, blur,
static and transient ecological interference into a
>memory with the frame built in.

(from "Pollen" by Mei-mei Berssenbrugge)

In Berssenbrugge's "Pollen," we encounter the person actively feeling its way, at the site of a spatio-temporal unfolding and creation. The long line in their various enjambments, excursions, and digressions tenuously hold together temporal and spatial percepts as they are actively felt through various referential frames—the frame of the spring, the frame of the body, the frame of memory. Such that a moment of order, both recognized and felt, happens as we encounter the only end-stopped line in this initial section of the poem, when sound coincides with sense, in the line/sentence: "Everything's in the field to designate and stabilize, plants evenly spaced by water."

"In-depth seriality takes time," the person in "Pollen" says, and also takes this time with "blur, static and transient ecological interference into a memory with the frame built in"—acknowledging that representations of perception not only take some time to find a form, but also that in the time that this coming into form happens, representations lose the noisy properties that come with perception-as-perception, the newness found in the duration between the initial encounter with landscape and the fuller ,stabilized reception of it, as the landscape is committed to memory, and fitted into a memory with a familiar configuration, i.e. with "the frame built in."

Poems are "gifted only with a feeble outer power," Mallarmé writes in his essay "Limited Action". "I have nothing to do with the poet," he declares: "perjure your verse." Yet despite the Mallarméan injunction, poets continue to write and read poems. Perhaps it is because we have come to accept that the poem's power is indeed feeble if one looks at it from the point of causing mass action and bringing about wider social change.

Poetry, I think, is not a service. But is, as Badiou says, an art, and therefore a process of truth. By exploring the minimal power of the line in reconfiguring our relationship to time and hence to the sensible world, I hope that we regain confidence in this minimal power. Such re-configurings to me are becoming more and more urgent and necessary, a necessity whose surface I can only scratch here.

Here and elsewhere our experience of time is mediated by empire: as monetized data through various social media, and platform- think business models, or as outsourced time with follow-the- sun models that "follow the sun" of global capital. I hope that in turning to the line, we are reminded that we must pursue and generate choices, a relationship with time, outside our given chronologies.

PIECES

I want to begin, sincerely, by admitting that the prospect of talking about my own book makes me feel uneasy. We say things about work we have written and find that in further thought, what we say it is, it is not; or we find what we speak of, and are frustrated to find little of anything else. So I will not talk about [my book] *they day daze*, it is what it is (which I am certain, and also hope, as with any poetic text, differs for each of us that reads it). What I want to do instead is to remember encounters, chance meetings, associations – which somewhat led to the making of *they day daze*. All of which it is not.

> I have tried to keep
> context from claiming you.

I quote these lines not from Keith Waldrop's *Transcendental Studies*, but from the website of the National Book Foundation where, in 2009, I first read them. Before that, I had not really engaged with Waldrop's work. I was more familiar with, and preferred the work of his wife, Rosmarie Waldrop, whose sentence-swerves in *Lawn of Excluded Middle*, I found most exciting. But I felt something in my sensibility change as I read Keith Waldrop:

> Balancing. Austere. Life-
> less. I have tried to keep
> context from claiming you.

There is something in these lines which distills many of the hopes and failures that a poet goes through in his writing practice. I have a vague memory of someone asking me: "can we still speak of essences?" I take that he asks not out of nostalgia for essentialist thought, but out of a frustration with prevailing modes of thinking and writing, in the social, linguistic, postmodern turn. Badiou says of postmodern and analytic thought, and I paraphrase, that they reflect the physiognomy of the world too much, that they are too compatible with the world to sustain the rupture that thought requires.

Also from Keith Waldrop:

"Now there is a door and whoever
very beautiful and very
very strange. Near you a table.

Laughing. Singing. Calling to one
another, the crack of whips. Cloud to
cloud in ricochet.

Music of hooves and wheels. The heavenly
Jerusalem from shards of Babylon
destroyed. Now a door.

Where thinking ends, house and temple
echo, possible objects of
admiration. Will you go?"

And whoever/ very beautiful and very/ very strange.

―――

On my last night in Paris, I decided to leave my camera in the apartment, to not take pictures with my phone. I felt that I wanted to just take a walk. This was on May 6, 2011. On the second floor of Shakespeare and Co., a woman with a yellow, feather scarf wrapped around her neck approached me and asked, "Are you Vietnamese?"

"No, I'm Filipino," I say.

"Filipino! My Uncle's wife is Filipina. I am a Dane, do you know any Danes?"

This was before I started taking serious interest in the sport of badminton. I will learn, a few months later, of the many top-ranked Danish badminton players at the international level. So I said, "Inger Christensen?"

"Yes," she said, adding "There are only two Danes you need to know. Inger Christensen and Khir-kegar."

"Khir-kegar?" I asked.

"Yes, Khirkegar."

"Oh, you mean Soren? Soren Khir-kegar," I copy her pronunciation.

"Yes, Kierkegaard," then she walked towards her companion—a bearded man wearing a top hat—who I imagined to be a French New Wave director. Then they left.

I happened upon a side-street I had never seen before. There were shops selling potato chips and beignets. There were women dressed in mini-skirts, and wearing bunny-ear headbands. There was a bar with a ceiling fan, with underwear hung on its fan-blades and the fan-blades turned. Then I saw again the Dane and her companion, who I recall carried with her—on the right hand a cane, on the left hand what seems to be a director's chair.

———

Image courtesy of the author, 2011.

This is the only digital collage in *they day daze*. I took a picture of a street, though I don't remember if it was from Strasbourg or Paris: *a street/ familiar for its street-like quality*. I do remember that the sky is a Googled image of the French newspaper *Le Monde. Le Monde*—the world.

When Derrida said "*Il n'ya pas de hors-texte*," I no longer imagined an inescapable language-world, a sky even, with nothing but language, but something which relates to the beauty of contexts. When I see things, when one sees objects as language, it is a language where something can emerge out of traces. One attempts to lift pieces from context, *to try to keep context from claiming* a "you," but the pieces carry with them traces, and the traces, glowing at the torn edges in a collage, become different pieces. I think that one can also replace pieces with an *I*, or a *he*, or a *she*, or with *we*.

Image courtesy of the author, 2011.

If I remember correctly, the image of the floating Buddha is from a leaflet from Starbucks, something that has to do with teas. The yellow tape from the crime scene is from the front-page of the *Philippine Star*. To form the scene of the crime, I cut out one of the happily playing girls. The girls do not notice Godzilla. I didn't get Godzilla from stills of the movie, but from an invitation to one of the artist-collagists, Dina Gadia's shows.

I think that I wanted some of my collage pieces to produce sentences.

Sentence: The girls happily on a tree cannot act upon the violence beside and behind it.

Image courtesy of the author, 2009.

I am sure that I remember this right—the elephant, the handcuffed hands, and the magician's hat are from a book on the life of Harry Houdini. The textual elephant is from a page which describes Harry Houdini's death, "collapsed offstage."

Sentence: An elephant is made of ideas, text, rococo; while all we know of birds is that while they are made of colors, some are from a magician's hat.

When Derrida said "Il n'ya pas de hors-texte," I think of Gertrude Stein's Room, a room, a world even where *Europe and Asia and being overbearing,* a sky from which we find *a light in the moon.* From Stein:

> A light in the moon the only light is on Sunday. What was the sensible decision. The sensible decision was that notwithstanding many declarations and more music, not even notwithstanding the choice and a torch and a collection, notwithstanding the celebrating hat and a vacation and even more noise than cutting, notwithstanding Europe and Asia and being overbearing, not even notwithstanding an elephant and a strict occasion, not even withstanding more cultivation and some seasoning, not even with drowning and with the ocean being encircling, not even with more likeness and any cloud, not even with terrific sacrifice of pedestrianism and a special resolution, not even more likely to be pleasing. The care with which the rain is wrong and the green is wrong and the white is wrong, the care with which there is a chair and plenty of breathing. The care with which there is incredible justice and likeness, all this makes a magnificent asparagus, and also a fountain.

Image courtesy of the author, 2009.

If I remember right, here I was thinking about the idea of surprise and the possibility of a parenthetical surprise. Is it possible to be surprised by a parenthesis? Again, from Stein: "Surprise, the only surprise has no occasion. It is an ingredient and the section the whole section is one season."

Sentence: I was thinking about the idea of surprise when it struck me that although the horse was surprised to come across parentheses (what then is a parenthetical surprise?) No one was worried about the swimmer rending the horse apart in the green blaze.

R.d.B.

"These days shall be my poems"
-- John Wieners

Image courtesy of the author, 2009.

I am certain that I got the sudoku background from a Kriss Kringle in the office. I am too lazy to solve puzzles, so I go straight to the last pages to cut out the answers.

"These days shall be my poems" comes from John Wiener's notebook published as *The Journal of John Wieners is to be called 707 Scott Street for Billie Holiday*. But I quote this from an issue of the literary journal *Conjunctions* where I first read excerpts from Wiener's notebook. There is a fascinating story behind his notebook's publication: One day, visiting Wiener's apartment, Lewis Warsh sees a trunk filled with notebooks and thinking out loud, says "I'd love to read them some day." Wieners got one of the notebooks, seemingly at random, and handed it to Warsh.

I go back to the issue of *Conjunctions* to read excerpts from "707 Scott Street." Then I read that it was not only Warsh who visited Wieners on that day. "In 1972, William Corbett and I visited John in his apartment at 44 Joy Street in Boston with the hope of getting poems from him for our magazine," Warsh writes of the event. So I remembered only two people in a room where there should have been three.

I once met someone who told me she had been to Moscow all by herself, who told me she had explored the city, with no Russian, only toting a Russian-to-French dictionary with her. If my memory serves me right, her name was Mirana, originally from Madagascar, who one day in the office (though I completely forget the context) was telling me "ca-hi-yey," who said, "how to say...?" who asked her boss, Philippe, "*Philippe*, what's ca-hi-yey."

"*Notebook*," Phillipe says.

Oh, "cahier," I say it back.

There are people you meet only once in your life. There is a beautiful short story by Lydia Davis titled "The Walk," where a translator and a critic meet at a Proust conference. It ends with the critic bidding goodbye to the translator with something like, "We will probably not meet again." There are people like Mirana, and Philippe whom I know I will probably not meet again.

In an attempt to remember encounters—people, pieces, a piece of day, a foreign word, et cetera, one finds that as in Jack Spicer, "Things do not connect; they correspond." Spicer who supposedly on his deathbed said, "My vocabulary did this to me."

The last fragment I would like to talk about is of the poet Kokoy Guevara, whom I first met some months after the publication of *they day daze*; whom I met only two other times before he passed away, but with whom I have had some deeply engaged conversations on poetry with — conversations, which at one point, he described in an email as "belligerent." Kokoy, who I mistakenly remember reading Cesar Vallejo's "I know a man mutilated," when I first met him at a reading. And who, in an email later on, corrects me: "I didn't read Vallejo. What was the title or line/s you remembered? I read Lacaba, Crane, Dickinson, Spicer, Hopkins and Berrigan."

But I vividly remember him giving a line-perfect reading of Spicer's "Thing Language":

> This ocean, humiliating in its disguises
> Tougher than anything.
> No one listens to poetry. The ocean
> Does not mean to be listened to. A drop
> Or crash of water. It means
> Nothing.
> It
> Is bread and butter
> Pepper and salt. The death
> That young men hope for. Aimlessly
> It pounds the shore. White and aimless signals.
> No One listens to poetry.

In memory of Kokoy, I would like to end with silence.

"So silence is pictorial/when silence is real" says Barbara Guest. So I will end with collage. I don't remember the sources of most of the pieces in this collage, but the musical notations are from a hardcopy of a score of John Cage's 4'33". One should notice that there are no notes on the staff, only whole rests, if one looks a little closely.

Sentence: From the phonograph, a waterfall, dragonflies now, folded flowers, now a chair—all these come crashing at 4'33" where one hears, now, the uneasy twitching of a nose in the string section.

Image courtesy of the author, 2014.

LYRIC GESTURE

Near them a tall man with thick chestnut hair held his left wrist as if it might be in pain. It was the intensity of his eyes that caught Kafka's attention more than his tall leanness which, from the evidence about, marked the aeronaut and the mechanic. This was the age of the birdman and of the magician of the machine. Who knows but what one of these preoccupied faces might belong to Marinetti himself? This was a crane of a man. The very wilderness of his curly brown hair and the tension in his long fingers seemed to speak of man's strange necessity to fly. He was talking to a short man in a mechanic's blue smock and with an eye-patch. From his mouth flew the words Kite Flying Upper Air Station, Höhere Luftstazion zum Drachensteigenlassen. Then the small man raised his square hands and cocked his head in a question. Glossop, was the answer, followed by the green word Derbyshire.
[...]
Otto squared his shoulders and approached a man who was obviously both an Italian and a reporter.

—Informazione, per favore, he said with a flamboyance Max and Franz had thought he used only upon the waiters of Prague. The reporter's eyes grew round and bright.
—Per essempio?
—Chi è il aviatore colà, prego?

—È Ruggiero. Francese.
—Ask him, Franz said, if he knows who that tall man is with the deep eyes and chestnut hair.
—E quest'uomo di occhi penetrante e capigliatura riccia? The reporter did not know. [...]
Otto gave the page to Franz.
—There's the name of the man you asked about, he said. He wrote it down for the giornalista.
Kafka looked at the name. It read, in light pencil, the kind meticulous men used to jot down fractions and the abbreviated titles of learned journals, volume, number, and page, probably a thin sliver pencil with fine lead, Ludwig Wittgenstenstein.
—Who? Max said.

The foregoing excerpt is from Guy Davenport's "The Aeroplanes at Brescia" first collected in his book of short fiction, *Tatlin!* then later selected as part of his short story collection *Twelve Stories*. "The Aeroplanes at Brescia" gives us Franz Kafka as he witnesses the air show in the Italian town of Brescia with his friends Max and Otto Brod. This momentous occasion in the history of aviation, the first international competition for airplanes, bannered a number of pioneers, among them Louis Bleriot, famous for making the first flight across the English Channel, Glenn Curtiss, and Henri Rougier. Davenport makes it a fictively wondrous event, engineering an unknowing meeting between Franz Kafka and Ludwig Wittgenstein, way before we referred to a particular mode of phantasmagoric fiction as *Kafkaesque*, and before we described language games—the tautological utterances of analytic philosophy—as *Wittgensteinian*. The story ends with a scene between Max Brod and Franz Kafka:

—Franz! Max said before he considered what he was saying, why are there tears in your eyes?
—I don't know, Kafka said. I don't know.

Franz Kafka, of course, will eventually be recognized as a major figure in modern literature; and Max Brod, Kafka's friend and biographer, a considerably prolific author in his own right, will later on be regarded more widely as the literary executor who ignored Kafka's instructions to burn his works after his death.

More than the wonderful meeting of proper names in what is an inarguably important event, what continues to draw me to this story is how intricately it unfolds a particular fascination, an inarticulability even, that happens when people encounter something significant happening before them but cannot describe what that thing is yet.

Davenport locates the proper names—Franz Kafka, Max Brod, Ludwig Wittgenstein—in that space between the proper and the common name, that allows persons to share in the glow of an ineffable, a collective recognition of a not-understanding. And for Kafka, in this story set in Brescia, there were two events: the air show with the rowdiness of its crowds, the bustle of its mechanics, and the grace of its aviators but also the private event with this stranger who kept holding on "to his left wrist as if it might be in pain," who had such intensity in his eyes: "I don't know, Kafka said, I don't know," Davenport writes. And with that sleight-of-hand, the person whose proper name is indeed Kafka, is before us (and also before Max), a teary-eyed Franz faced with the inarticulable.

Before it was the title of Davenport's short story, "The Aeroplanes at Brescia" was the title of an editorial by Franz Kafka published in the Sept 29, 1909 issue of the Prague-based,

German newspaper *Bohemia*. In 1909, Wittgenstein was in fact studying aeronautics at the University of Manchester with a research focus on the flying of kites. Twenty-five years later, in a journal entry, he would write, "I think I summed up my position vis-à-vis philosophy when I said: Philosophy should really be written only as one would write poetry."

———

In Davenport's film, I find an aleatory notion of speculative meetings which creates the contingency of lives intersecting, even though improbably, even if only tangentially. This brings me to consider a particular manner of composition. Instead of exposition or narrative, I want to consider composing poems as if through a series of gestures; to see what gestures can become if they do not become exposition, what they make of exposition; to see how facts, persons, and anecdotes can be shaped in the composition by replacing setting with the duration and space of prosody and the page; to see how bringing people into the page's field of attention allows for accident and chance.

At the risk of saying something over-determined, it is *gesture* that allows for person to activate contingency in a poem. And perhaps the *I* and its *other*, the *we* and their articulations are themselves gestures—in the sense that is close to Agamben's description of gesture as a "communication of a communicability," a "being- in-language"—as a "gesture of not being able to figure something out in language." I use 'gesture' here less to mean something like a surface action, but more to mean the involuntary, what is still within, but exceeds intention—only to be indicated through gesture itself

Gestures can be empty in the realm of thought and also in the sphere of action. When gesture is read as pure mediality, it is both means and end. When gesture ceases to open up possibility, it is stuck in something like an ineffectual, and purely tautological postmodernist play on difference. In the empty political gesture, when gesture is a matter of appearances, it is precisely because it *appears* to but does not actually achieve the good it purports to accomplish.

"Politics is the sphere of pure means, that is, of the absolute and complete gesturality of human beings," writes Agamben, in recognition of its dialectic potential. I think it is the gestural that enlivens form, that allows form to respond to the present, which keeps the openness of form and prevents it from becoming codified as mannerism. I seek a composition that produces gestures, in which mediality is not gesture's absolute end, but as a method such that mediality can remain as just that—means as means—in unfolding, patient, inexhaustible approximations.

One artist's practice corresponds to the events of their life, bounces off, echoes the practice and life of another in inexhaustible reverberations and finite aspects, which I hope to recirculate in poems. Take for example Agnes Martin's idea of joy or Guy Debord's Situationist instructions for a dèrive; the various spaces for friendships as produced in the collage practice of Kurt Schwitters, and in the performance work of On Kawara; the virtual site where labor and dream intersect in the anarchitectural work of Gordon Matta-Clark, and the unconventionally scored music of Toru Takemitsu.

―――

Construction," Walter Benjamin quotes Siegfried Giedon in Convolute K of the Arcades projects, "plays the role of the subconscious." Bright moments between an instant and attention. We seek immediacy by hewing as close as possible to design. Gesture means defective products haphazardly, daily, slipping past, forever, from our fingers. But gesture is a dream, and dailiness the sheen about our dream objects, about our longue duree.

———

In a lecture delivered before his audience in Tokyo's Studio 200 in 1984, Toru Takemitsu said, "The title of my work," referring to his orchestral composition *A Flock Descends into a Pentagonal Garden*, "is based on a strange dream." He continued:

> The same spring in which I received a commission from the San Francisco Symphony Orchestra, there was a large retrospective show of works by Marcel Duchamp at the Centre Pompidou in Paris. I feel my dream was influenced by a portrait of Duchamp by Man Ray included in that exhibit. The photograph shows Duchamp's head with a star shape shaved on its own.
>
> The night after seeing that photo I dreamt of a pentagonal garden. Flying down and into the garden were countless white birds led by a single black bird. I rarely dream; perhaps that is why the impression left was so strong. When I awoke, that landscape felt very musical, and I wanted to turn it into a composition. For a long time afterward I relived the dream, making precise notes of the memories it evoked. The title somehow emerged: A Flock Descends into the Pentagonal Garden.

From Takemitsu, there is a possible manner of incorporating dream material in the work. The dream material folded, unfolded, re-folded, while maintaining its dialectical quality, without forcing it to become meaning or content. In Takemitsu's case: to "clarify musically through something as simple as numbers." I also think about the generative potential of dreams. On the importance of dreams and the "figurative status of awakening" in Walter Benjamin's *Arcades Project*, the scholar and thinker Alexander Gelley writes: "In transposing the Freudian dream work from the individual subject to the collective, Benjamin projected a 'macrocosmic journey' of the individual sleeper to the 'dreaming collective, which through the arcades, communes with its own insides.'"

Work and dream, in the lyric imagination, is the palpable atmosphere of prosody. Prosody as gesture, as both the inescapable in speech, is the configurable material in poems. And in what ways can gesture, dream content, the lyric intersection of lives make possible an imagining that is the opposite of a formless phantasmagoria?

There is a beautiful scene in Theo Angelopolous's *Eternity and a Day* where the terminally ill protagonist Alexander plays music from his room. The phonograph music spills out into the neighborhood space by way of his balcony. He plays the same music each day, and every time he does, his neighbor from the second-floor room, in a building across from his, responds to him by playing the exact same music back. This scene contains the tenuous but thoroughly sincere connection between two persons made possible by music, between Alexander and the neighbor whom he does not personally know.

"For the last few months," Alexander tells us, "My only contact with the world has been this unknown neighbor of mine, who always answers to me with the same music. Who are they? What are they like? One morning I want to go and meet them, but then I changed my mind. Maybe it's better not to meet them and imagine them. Will it be a hermit like me? Or perhaps a little girl, who before leaving for school, plays with the unknown neighbor."

SO FACTURE IS THE MATERIAL FACT OF JOY

It is the fifth of April 1976. As an alternative to concrete response, which can be violent, and to transcendent response, which can be detached, Agnes Martin speaks of an abstract response. "We are in the midst of reality," she says, "responding with joy."

It is the seventeenth of May 1961. For the *Research Group on Everyday Life*, Guy Debord clicks on his tape recorder which begins to deliver his prerecorded lecture.

But while everyone agrees on the being of reality, Debord needs to insist on the existence of everyday life, despite the sociologists.

Can we say that this altering of our experience of a lecture is responding with joy?

In Agnes Martin, the experience of joy is elusive because it is rare.

In Guy Debord, we find life that is structured by the scarcity of free time.

It is everyday life which gives reality and joy a palpability. A sociality which renders the unlikely union of Agnes and Guy in a sentence: We are in everyday life responding with joy — an experience that is scarce and rare.

This sentence requires a studio where we can wait, or where we can walk —

A willed reception, a radical waiting; we wait for falling blue;

Or we walk up a fire exit because the rusting on its rails appears like a cloud of burnt sienna, a radiating color field, then we find a satellite dish. We break away from our dérive, each with the task of bringing back a microwave oven.

For elusiveness, attention.

For scarcity, choice and risk.

So Martin's *Gabriel* is attentively looking at the virtual from the actual, and seeing, for 78 minutes through the beach and the mountains, horizontal bands of color. While in Debord's *La Société du Spectacle*, it is montage after montage of text spliced to image that forms a spectacular whole.

We can trace a common thread of generosity running in these studios. When Agnes Martin speaks of joy, it is joy factured in everyday life.

R.d.B.

An "awareness

of the profound richness and energy abandoned in everyday life inseparable"

from an "awareness
of the poverty of the dominant organization of this life."

So we quote Guy Debord.

But Agnes cautions us on the experience of others: we are "in reality at a standstill, because their experience is in the past."

Which is why we respond with the lyric,

and in choosing the lyric, live with a text long enough, attentively enough, to begin to imagine for it, more than this experience, a prosody, a text inscribed in present time.

This requires a studio, where we can cite and quote, that persists in the present. Citation as site, and facture as the material fact of joy.

Grids

to mark that we have located something which we cannot possess; that is not knowledge; we are happy.

Grids unquote.

t.d.o.a.c.t.i.e.

For morning, for falling blue, for loving love

for earnestly pondering slight alterations of usual procedures

the everyday right here   How

is our life

ACTION, NUMBER, SILENCE, WORK
10.13.2017

The situations of a life, however they may call for a response, prove none of the responses adequate. I think here of George Oppen, his silence for 25 years, between *Discrete Series* and *The Materials*; of Simon Hantaï, his silence for 16 years; but also of the aura that their silences, such silences seem to gather—an aura that is to a certain extent, a kind of preciousness, an unproductive reverence—

But today what draws me to their silences are neither the speculations on the causes of their silences, nor accounts of the lives they led in those silent years. (Oppen's political work, Hantaï's refusal to participate in the art market, facts of life gathered from letters, accounts of friends...) I think that what draws me in today are the changes in the sensibilities that come after such silences, how work might proceed after a radical pause.

This shift in sensibility is marked in Oppen's lines, his sentences, and the corresponding tensions between them. His lines in *The Materials* are markedly composed to be *less* unravelments of precise Imagist units, and *more* formal support to what seems like a consciousness (personal, collective) as it works through the structures of what it means to be human. An *I* or *we* are bound by, yet never fully determined, by the poem's inner realities or its external world. "What will she make of a world/ Do you suppose, Max, of which she is made," he writes in the poem "Sara in Her Father's Arms" from *The Materials*.

Simon Hantaï withdrew from his art practice in 1982 as a response to Greenbergian art criticism, and the frivolousness of the art market. "Our only defense is to refuse to participate," his friend the gallerist Paul Rodgers recalled him saying. In 1998, he broke his silence with two major paintings: *Laissée* and *Travaux de lecture*. Hantaï created his *Laissée* series (*Leftover* series) by unearthing then cutting-up *Tabula*, a large-scale pliage work which he had previously destroyed.

Meanwhile, *Travaux de lecture* was created by request of his friend Jean-Luc Nancy to serve as the frontispiece for Nancy's book on Jacques Derrida. In *Travaux*, Hantaï copied texts from both Nancy and Derrida then wrote and re-wrote over these texts on stiffened and crumpled batiste until the resulting "manuscripts" became unreadable. This method of painting characterized by its palimpsestic procedures had been prefigured by another of Hantaï's earlier work called *Ecriture Rose*.

From 1958 to 1959, Hantaï worked every morning on *Ecriture Rose*, copying texts from Hegel, Nietzsche, Hölderlin, Freud, the Bible, writing dates of his own life, writing over and over using green, black, and blue paint until the color rose emerged from the canvas. In March 2000, he mailed *Travaux* to Jean-Luc Nancy, living inStrasbourg at the time, as a gift.

R.d.B.

What is accomplished through writing is the color rose

Beginning green, beginning black. Hegel: *In making
its inorganic nature organic
to himself,*

and taking possession of it for himself. Looked at, however,

Ending black. Maintains the missing. And the quiet is the fold.

While the word does not mean
or means
only itself

Word is where the work turns
Is read as color is relation

So the work
in the economy of the gift must be held in relation
may be word

———

I am drawn to a particular poem by Paul Celan for its many silences. If silence is—where the silences are—understood as the pause necessary to meaningfully proceed with the work, then Celan's silences are highly productive.

"Port-bau - Deutsch?" was written in 1959, between "Sprachgitter" and "Die Niemandsrose" but only saw publication much later on, after Celan's death. It is a poem that speaks with Walter Benjamin. Port-bau is where Benjamin took his own life in Sept 1940 after being refused entry into Spain—

Benjamin, whose thinking of the "aura" was a precise articulation of the changes happening to the sensibility of his time – changes in response to transformations in the period's sensorium spurred then conditioned by the event of mechanical reproduction—

Celan, and the marked shift in the structure of his work beginning in "Sprachgitter" and gaining full articulation in "Atemwende:" his shift to the word, to the "turn in breath," to that space between breathing in then breathing out as the main unit of poetic composition —

———

I search for an attempt I made at translating "Port-bou" in my notebook of 2015. An attempt, which I remember making, and only barely making, with my limited German, a dictionary, and numerous secondary texts; an attempt I made because I was then unable to find an English translation, but was really keen on reading this particular Celan poem which I knew very well spoke with Walter Benjamin. A couple of months later, I was able to read an English translation by Ian Fairley emailed to me by my friend A.

I find myself working on another translation attempt today:

Port-bou – German?
Arrow the stealth cloak off, the
steel helmet.

Left   –
Nibelungs, Right –
Nibelungs:

Rhined, purified
overburden.

Benjamin
no-one you, for ever,
the yes-sayer.

Such heroic era, even
as B-Bauhaus:
no.

Not a too-late,
a secret
open.

As with a good number of Celan's poems, "Port-bau – Deutsch?" is replete with allusions: Wagner's *Nibelungen*, the Rhine crisis and the increased German nationalism that it brought about (also the corresponding *ressentiment*), fragments taken from Walter Benjamin's essay "Against a Masterpiece," and perhaps many other references to be found should one mine both the main text and the multitude of secondary materials. But I think what continually draws me to work on a translation of "Port-bau – Deutsch?" is not the prospect of an exegesis, but rather the chance to revisit that almost inarticulable sense of place, that vertiginous teetering on an in-between language, the geographic boundaries of Port-bau and the Rhine, the affirmation possible in the negative via Benjamin's refugee status—his being a "no- one," the secret open, the stuttering that says to the propaganda of German greatness given support from its "heroic era" to the time of the Bauhaus: "No."

Simon Hantaï to Jean-Luc Nancy:

> I'm coming to a first stage of saturation that I've already told you about. There are thresholds of saturation, tidelines. Time passes, I write, nothing seems to move. But soon signs appear (strokes accumulating on one another, next to one another, heading toward marks, toward another picturality).

Jacques Maritain by way of George Oppen:
> We awake in the same moment to ourselves and to things.

R.d.B.

10.31.2017

(draft—translation—from Allan Popa's *Modus Operandi*):

2
Which poet will hazard
to say that he is no different
that to make is to work
when no relief comes
through the structure built on the page
despite many rooms.

There are structures built
so that no one goes to sleep
because the yearning of money does not sleep
in the market, the pawnshop, the bank.

If it can be uttered
believably
I want to believe
that what flows through a poem is the opposite
of the language of commerce because
of its powerlessness to effect.
There is nothing gained
in the surplus of meaning.

Even though the path of capital
is boundless transformation
though nothing is changed.

———

I remember receiving my copy of *Modus Operandi* from Allan Popa himself in the BLTX[1] small press expo in Ilyong's. I ask him for a copy, and he pulls out a slim, orange chapbook from his bag. *Modus Operandi* consists of poems by Allan Popa, and drawings by Ruzzel Valdepeña. The drawings, whose thick dark lines are reminiscent of woodcut prints, are of hands wielding various work tools. The poem's lines have the quality of an unfolding perception, which is not quite like the poetic line when it emulates the sensible world becoming knowledge, but more like the poetic line when it carries with it both aesthetic and ethical weight.

In the case of *Modus Operandi*, this ethical-aesthetic weight is manifest in the (dis)entanglement of word with work. Work, in its sense as labor, and in the sense that Agamben highlights—work is, among man's various modes of actions, the most necessary to the biological process of life.

By translating Allan's work, when choices have to be made among multiple generative possibilities, readings, translations—is not translation a manner of reading? —one experiences this sense of phenomenology which bears both aesthetic and ethical weight.

Consider for instance the lines:

---

1. BLTX - Better Living Through Xeroxography Fair founded by Adam David and Chingbee Cruz, eventually expanding to a consortium of micropresses and individual creators, puts up spaces for creators working outside the circuits of mainstream publishing where creators gather, share, and work directly with readers. The general practice is more geared to DIY.

> Ano ang sibilasasyon
> kundi arkitektura
> ng pagbubukod ng tao
> sa hindi, ng loob sa labas
>
> Ang saysay
> ng mga hadlang
> ay kasaysayan.

Which I chose to translate as:

> What is civilization
> if not the architecture
> of separating man
> from what is not, inside from outside.
>
> The utterance
> of the barriers
> is history.

The first stanza itself already presents challenges: deciding on which article to use, keeping or leaving out prepositions, etc. But a more challenging set of choices needs to be made in the second stanza. "Kasaysayan" which directly translates to 'history,' has in it the word "saysay" which can mean any of 'value,' 'meaning,' 'statement,' ... For today, I choose to translate it as 'utterance.' With the intent to echo lines from the last section of the chapbook which go: "Bumibigay ang tula sa bigat/ ng sariling pahayag" ("The poem gives in to the weight/ of its own utterance"). And also in the attempt to foreground wordplay with work, with the proliferation of walls, buildings and ruins in *Modus Operandi*, of the immaterial "utterance" with the concrete "barriers."

———

(draft—translation—from Allan Popa's *Modus Operandi*)

3
The use of tools is beyond use.
What is new
in time
when the form that is made of that
which does not
easily give
has not changed.

The world does not
easily give.
This does not change.

The tools of the worker
forged by the history of work.

I believe
the city was built
of dream
so that dreaming
may proceed.

[...]

———

In "Poiesis and Praxis," Agamben writes about how "the distinction between these three kinds of doing—poiesis, praxis, and work—has been progressively obscured." In Greek thought, man's "doing" is any of Poiesis— "to pro-duce" in the sense of bringing something into being (from non-being to being); Praxis—"to do" in the sense of acting out, expressing the will; and Work—physical work necessary for life's needs.

He later goes on to discuss a shift in the status accorded to work throughout the history of western thought, and how work "climbs to the rank of central value [...] in every human activity." He reminds us that in Ancient thought, work occupies "the lowest rank in the hierarchy of active life, whereas in both the classical liberalism of John Locke and Adam Smith, and also the writings of Karl Marx, work attains something of a central value—in Locke and Smith, where work is, respectively, origin of property, and source of wealth; and in Marx, where work is the expression of man's very humanity.

In the realm of art, the disentangling of the categories of poiesis, praxis, and work, is essential. Agamben observes how in most contemporary art practices, art is interpreted as a mode of praxis, where praxis is "the expression of a will and a creative force." For Agamben, this "expressivist" mode of thought remains central even within what is otherwise deemed radical aesthetics: in Nietzsche's vision of the universe as "art that gives birth to itself," in Artaud's highly visceral, liberatory theater as a freeing from normative representation, and in the Situationists' "overcoming of art" that confuses between art (*poiesis*) and daily life (*praxis*).

Why is there a necessity to think again of art as poiesis, of art in relation to "pro-ducing," in the sense of bringing something to being? And how is it possible for such need to be real, without nostalgia for a metaphysical past?

Alain Badiou offers us a possible response. In Badiou, the event of art is "a new possibility of formalization, the becoming form of something that is not form... Because I think the political situation today is very obscure," Badiou says. "The specific responsibility of artistic creation is to help humanity find the new subjective paradigm."

I think the poems in *Modus Operandi* are aware of the necessity of disentangling the categories of poiesis, praxis, and work. But at the same time also deeply aware of how inevitably entangled these categories have become, of how the poem's powerlessness to effect change is both harrowing fact and potential. The poems recognize that "The unbeknownst/ is a border /is a passage only/ the small know about."

———

(draft—translation—from Allan Popa's *Modus Operandi*)

4
Teeth ache
from the gloss of the aluminum
of the iron case
of the head that needs to be covered
because more or less
you recognize the facelessness.

R.d.B.

The unbeknownst
is a border
is a passage only
the small know about.

*The void
is already in language,* says the termite.

*Find the means
when there is no way,*
the lizard on the ceiling, says in response,
upside-down
late at night.

*The poem gives in to the weight
of its own utterance,*
the ant avers.

*But the clock
only the clock
remains
with its hands clean.*

01.04.2018

Isn't a day a number—each of our days marked by the hyper-abundance of numbers? The day of the year, our monthly wages, the prices of basic necessities, casualties in the recent disaster, distances we travel to work, taxes, tax cuts; then the prices of the same basic commodities increase. Then apricot trees, says Inger Christensen:

> apricot trees exist, apricot trees exist

Number's power to be the arbiter of capital's laws, and also to define the forms that nature takes. Its and our persistence. And bracken:

> bracken exists; and blackberries, blackberries;
> bromine exists; and hydrogen, hydrogen

Reading Inger Christensen's *Alphabet*, moving along the stream of things in her lyric sequence, alphabetic and Fibonaccic, both—the repetitions, the capaciousness of her lines to include everything, and still not be excessive...

Badiou talking about Number: how the notion of infinity is revealed to thought as thought expands from the set of natural numbers to the set of rational numbers, how what used to be nothing, the void say, between the numbers 1 and 2 become infinity.

And Christensen, a world in these three lines:

> cicadas exist; chicory, chromium,
> citrus trees; cicadas exist;
> cicadas, cedars, cypresses, the cerebellum

R.d.B.

Today is Jan 4, 2018. 01-04-2018. A number names this day.

In the same talk, Badiou retells Plato's "Allegory of the Cave," this time the transition from the world of appearances to the world of reality is achieved, not with images but by science: arithmetic, specifically—quantities, distances, volumes—by numbers. In our contemporary cave, and I paraphrase Badiou, even the images are numbers: bits and pixels borne out of the pure difference and the well-orderedness of 0's and 1's.

Or perhaps, 52 years ago, On Kawara, painting Jan 4, 1966—the date in white font against the cerulean blue background—, attempted to formally unmake the digital image by painting numbers? Yet today, even the most inspired of gestures are suspect—for what does formal innovation in the visual arts accomplish when at Christie's, On Kawara's *Today Series* is auctioned in lots? A reminder to insist on the potency of art: in Badiou, the truth is something new, and at the reverse side of the abundance of capital is the rarity of the event of truth.

> doves exist, dreamers, and dolls;
> killers exist, and doves, and doves;
> haze, dioxin, and days; days
> exist, days and death; and poems
> exist; poems, days, death

We continue to insist on dreamers, despite dioxin and haze, on doves, on poems despite death, on poems, days, and death. Inger Christensen's *Alphabet* ends at section 14, with the letter "n." And there is something quite elegant in this design, something like the convergence of letter and number in the variable "n"—a letter quite frequently used to denote numbers.

05.27.2018

I had second thoughts in the bookshop on whether or not to get Simon Hanselmann's *Megahex*. Later on, decided, I went back and bought myself a copy. It seemed quite an interesting addition to the readings I have planned for later in the afternoon and towards evening. A reading list which I imagined to include Jacques Roubaud and his interpolations in *The Great Fire of London*, the sonnet sequence in Geoffrey G O'Brien's *Experience in Groups*, and Guy Davenport's short story on the Lascaux cave paintings.

So I headed back to the shop and left some of my things—a blue notebook, a 0.38pt black-blue pen, and Susan Howe's *That This*—with my friends K and A, at our table in the café. As I went out, I noticed that A flipped through pages of the Susan Howe.

When I got back, A said: "K and I were wondering how you would read this":

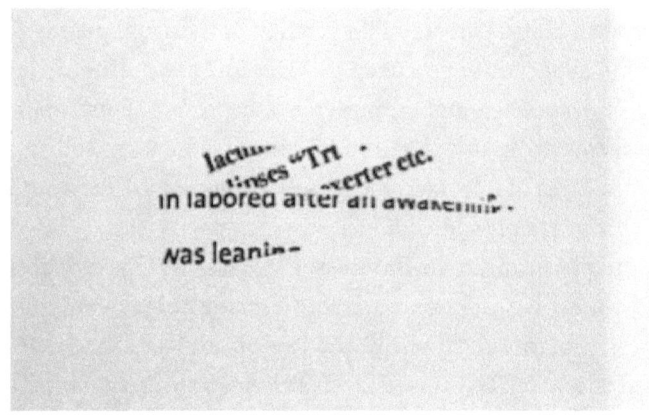

Image from *That This*, Susan Howe, 2010.

Half-jokingly, I made noises that contained L, T, W and several vowel sounds.

It is now late evening, and, giving more thought to the affairs of the day, I note that I chose to give the Howe collage a sound. Several things led to my choosing to give it a sound—*That This* is a poetry book, the specific collage section K and A read in the café is sandwiched between an prose chapter and a chapter of lineated verse, and obviously because I was asked: *how would you read this?* But now I also want to take note of illegibility;how collage, specifically those that work with language-material such as Susan Howe's, takes place in the overlap of the legible and the illegible—an illegibility pushed further as the textual becomes visual. Thinking about illegibility in this particular sense makes more apparent the limitations of thinking about (i.e. reading) visual work using structures modeled after language.

Even poems that are obviously not visual poetry still carry with them aspects of illegibility. If in visual poems the illegible aspect is introduced via the foregrounding of language's graphic elements, in verse and prose poems this aspect seems to be made through sound—when expectations one may have of normative logic are unmet, or are differently met through a prosodic logic.

"I placed a jar in Tennessee" writes Wallace Stevens "And round it was, upon a hill. /It made the slovenly wilderness/ Surround that hill" and it is quite clear that Stevens placed the jar in Tennessee for Tennessee's three syllables, its *s* followed by a long *e* sound, and for its particular distribution of stresses, as much for its hills and slovenly wilderness.

Or in an example from Lyn Hejinian, a prosodic and rhyming logic drives a semblance of a lyric I, so much that the didactic manner of saying which occurs in every third line, rather than being aphoristic, becomes a comedic slapstick made possible by rhyme:

> I thought I saw a rhubarb pie sitting on the stove
> Then I saw it was the tide receding from a cove
> But although I have strong emotions when I watch a movie, jealousy is never one of them.
>
> I thought I saw a bicyclist racing down the road
> Then I saw it was a note, a message still in code
> But sense is always either being raised to or lowered from the sky.
>
> I thought I saw a gourmet chef smear himself with cream
> Then I saw it was myself just entering a dream
> But we all know that the imagination when left to itself will brave anything

(from Lyn Hejinian's "The Book of A Thousand Eyes")

———

Last night, I dreamt I was in a gathering of friends[1]. People[2] were speaking with each other. I thought that they were simultaneously people and friends. In my mind in the dream, I knew them, but I was also aware that I didn't know any of them in waking life[3]. Then I woke up, and realized that in all the gestures of hands, and laughter, all the talk and nodding of heads, I didn't remember hearing any sound[4, 5].

1. "Reading shares this necessarily unsanctioned intimacy," writes Lisa Robertson "I have the strong sense that reading chooses me, as have my friendships.
2. From Agamben's "The Coming Community":
   What was most striking about the demonstrations of the Chinese May [Tiananmen], in fact, was the relative absence of specific content in their demands. (The notions of democracy and freedom are too generic to constitute a real goal of struggle, and the only concrete demand, the rehabilitation of Hu Yaobang, was promptly granted.) [...] In Tiananmen the state found itself facing something that could not and did not want to be represented, but that presented itself nonetheless as a community and as a common life (and regardless of whether those who were there in the square were actually aware of it.) The threat the state is not willing to come to terms with is precisely the fact that the unrepresentable should exist and form a community without either presuppositions or conditions of belonging (just like Cantor's inconsistent multiplicity). The whatever singularity—this singularity that wants to take possession of belonging itself as well as of its own being- into-language, and that thus declines any identity and any condition of belonging—is the new, nonsubjective, and socially inconsistent protagonist of the coming

politics. Wherever these singularities peacefully manifest their being-in-common, there will be another Tiananmen and sooner or later, the tanks will appear again.

3. The first section of *That This* is titled *Disappearance Approach*, where Susan Howe writes about her husband Peter Hare's death. Thinking about CS Peirce and the moment of her husband's death, she writes:

> It could have been the instant of balance between silence, seeing, and saying; the moment before speech. [CS] Peirce would call this moment, secondness. Peter was returning to the common course of things—our world of signs.

4. John Cage enters an anechoic chamber and hears two sounds: the electric buzz of his nervous system, and the beating of his own heart.

5. I remember another dream, one set in a very particular kind of light. It is a light that makes one doubt the realness of people and of things, a light that makes me doubt even the music that I hear, the one that is playing now.

R.d.B.

06.10.2018

I attempt today to continue to read and make art as a way of distracting myself from the weather. It is the second day of continual rains: weather that presents challenges to one's emotional disposition. I never had a fondness for the rains, especially today's kind. I think that my emotion in this weather has a chemical vis-à-vis material ground brought about by having lived a good number of my early years in a flood-prone area. I work on, then rework, a painting which I call "green is a difficult color." Green is a difficult color, and in this weather, the problem of not resembling trees.

In a chapter supposedly for his self- portrait from *The Great Fire of London*, Jacques Roubaud includes, after a section on his height ("I'm on the tall side"), then on his nose ("My nose is long"), the physical attributes: walker, swimmer, counter, and reader. I think about his self-portrait as *counter*, as *reader*, as I attempt to refocus my attention.

I will call these series of days, these writings marked by days *Leisure*. Leisure thought along the lines of Henri Lefevbre, its necessary relation to work and to our experience of the everyday. Leisure—because this reading and also this writing about what I read will almost always have a relationship to the everyday, to action, and to work.

Or maybe, I will call these days *Action, Number, Silence, Work*—the terms that constellate most of our days. "[T]here is no essence, no historical or spiritual vocation, no biological destiny that humans must enact or realize," writes Agamben. Otherwise, "no ethical experience would be possible-there would only be tasks to be done." A writing *through* of certain days presents a viable form for ethical experience, a possibility that is outside of tasks.

Agamben then introduces *potentiality* as a necessary third term, the ethical choice that one must make when faced with the options "to be" (i.e., the choice of the decisionist) or "to not-be" (i.e., the choice of the nihilist). "There is in effect something that humans are and have to be, but this something is not an essence nor properly a thing: *It is the simple fact of one's own existence as possibility or potentiality.*"

As with Agamben's other terms, I read *potentiality* and am not immediately or viscerally comforted. Although there seems to be something quite ideal, something inherently positive in thinking in terms of possibility, there is also something that verges on inaction, to the pitfalls of a reductive recourse to infinite deferral. But much like Agamben's other nuanced concepts: the "whatever," "gesture," etc. there is typically a lot to unfold, a lot to be furthered, and also a lot that Agamben later on revises from his initial determinations. But in what sense can this ethical choice remain in potentiality but still have consequence, or how can something pertinently exist without resulting from tidy, reductive notions of action or inaction?

Some initial thoughts, some corresponding examples, something towards an understanding:

1. In 1965, Roman Opalka decides to paint, with white pigment, numbers that would progress sequentially from one canvas to the next for the rest of his life. He calls his work *Detail*, and would later on include a black and white photograph of himself taken upon the completion of a day's work.

"It's important," Opalka says, "that my last *Detail* should not be finished by me, but my life."

2. I forget whom I paraphrase, but something about our continual working towards the good, without a full understanding of what the good is, but always challenging, progressing our sense of the ideal, our sense of the good. Isn't this the kind of uncertainty we call hope?

3. Emily Dickinson: "For Occupation - This -/ The spreading wide my narrow Hands/ To gather Paradise -"

07.07.2018

The multiple correspondences in thought between Agamben and Badiou, which I took note of as I read Agamben's "The Coming Community," reaches something like a reading denouement when on page 76, in the chapter titled "Homonyms," Agamben mentions Badiou himself: "*Whatever* does not therefore mean only (in the words of Alain Badiou) 'subtracted from the authority of language, without any possible denomination, indiscernible'; it means more exactly that which, holding itself in simple homonymy, in pure being called, is precisely and only for this reason unnamable: the being in language of the non-linguistic."

Prior to this chapter, I already took note of various linkages in their thoughts: a shared reference to Cantorian set theory (particularly the aporias brought to life through Russell's paradox, i.e., the set of all sets that do not exclude themselves), the role of the "State" in diminishing political action, et cetera. On a different day, and perhaps via a rather circuitous path, I think that I may, and through a more focused attempt, find ideational links between Agamben's reading of St. Thomas' treaties on halos, and Badiou's ideas on small and large infinities and their relation to the becoming of truth.

But for today I pursue the reading denouement at hand, and find a transcript of a seminar by Badiou where Agamben was among the interveners. The post-lecture intervention follows:

> **Giorgio Agamben:** I want to ask you a question about the limit point of the unnamable. We might recall the axiom of the white knight in 'Alice through the Looking

R.d.B.

Glass'. You remember that the white knight says that we have no name for the name. The thing for which we lack names is the name itself. This goes with what Heidegger says in a certain way, that we have no word for the saying of language itself. It seems to be in that perspective that the point you call unnamable is a strange point in which language and real in a way coincide. The thing for which we have no name is language itself.

Alain Badiou: Yes, I prefer your second formulation, that the point is something like a point where the real and nomination are not really separated. The proper of the proper, the pure real, but the pure real is something which is indiscernible to the pure word as well. I agree with the conviction that under the unnamable you have a real point, but its relation to language is absolutely irreducible. So not exactly the name for name, because it is lack of name, not lack of name for name, but lack of name for something like the real of the real, the absolute real of the complete field.

Critical differences are brought to light through this intervention. For Agamben, the *whatever*—his version of Badiou's *unnamable*—is a quotidian given. It is "the name for the name." Agamben remarks, in further elucidation of the point, that when we try to grasp the concept as such, the concept is "fatally transformed into an object and the price we pay is that we are no longer able to distinguish the concept from the conceived thing." He cites a commonplace example: when we try to grasp the concept of, say, a "shoe" it becomes impossible to distinguish this concept from the object that is the shoe.

For Badiou, however, the *unnamable* designates a more particular subset of a situation. It is that which the situation cannot name, or one that a situation attempts to name albeit with disastrous consequences. The *unnamable* is the limit of the "power of a truth." It is what is "forcibly" named when, say, in the realm of politics, we have totalitarianism, or when in the realm of science, we have something like the desire for the "omnipotence" of scientific truths.

I think, and despite the apparent inconsistencies, that Agamben and Badiou's ideas occur at two variously intersecting worlds: Badiou's in a neo-Platonic, his material world is marked by the occurrence of rare events which revolutionary subjects must latch on to, then see through; Agamben's in a spiritual-material, Walter-Benjaminian world that finds messianic potential in fragments of the quotidian. In a chapter from "The Coming Community," Agamben quotes Benjamin's recollection of a messianic parable, which Benjamin in turn recalls hearing from Gershom Scholem:

> The *Hassidim* tell a story about the world to come that says everything there will be just as it is here. Just as our room is now, so it will be in the world to come; where our baby sleeps now, there too it will sleep in the other world. And the clothes we wear in this world, those too we will wear there. Everything will be as it is now, just a little different.

If my memory serves me right, I think Foucault once said that one should never stop with thought, or rather that thought must continue through with action, that action is not merely the proving ground of thought, but rather and also the intensification of thinking. I think about these now and somehow make sense of the solace I find whenever I encounter correspondences in thinking, correspondences such as in Agamben and in Badiou's, in the idea of at least two people, hence a minimum of community, in synonymous pursuit of better possibilities of world.

07.24.2018

... again, Oppen.

A couple of days back, my friend A noticed that I was reading George Oppen again. This was over late lunch, when I had beside me, on the chair, the second book of Jason Lutes's *Berlin* and Oppen's *New Collected Poems* edited by Michael Davidson. *But we never leave Oppen*, was maybe something I said, or perhaps I replied with something like, *But don't we always go back to Oppen?*, knowing how much Oppen continues to sustain each of our writings, and in turn sustains each of us.

Who was it that said that poetry does not provides answers, but instead generates new questions, and that great poetry is poetry where both question and answer are intricately bound? Oppen pursued a great question, the "meaning of being numerous" which "we have chosen," a question whose becoming is bound with the becoming of the individual in the face of the grand, or rather and more precisely, the monstrous collectives: of nation-states and wars, of corporations and systematic violence; man's becoming in modernity, modernity which Arendt characterized by the dissolution of the public and the private spheres, the emergence of labor and bureaucracies, of mass societies and the manipulation of public opinion.

Whereas Arendt's genius was in building an analytic language for examining these confounding realities, Oppen's was in pursuing the question towards the intimate spaces that language creates (is this possibly the meaning of contemporary lyrical space?), the space where language as a semantic field meets language as a possible unfolding of our very human condition.

1
There are things
We live among 'and to see them
Is to know ourselves'

Occurrence, a part
Of an infinite series,
The sad marvels;

Of this was told
A tale of our wickedness.
It is not our wickedness.

'You remember that old town we went to, and we sat in the ruined window, and we tried to imagine that we belonged to those times – It is dead and it is not dead, and you cannot imagine either its life or its death; the earth speaks and the salamander speaks, the Spring comes and only obscures it –

Thus famously begins *Of Being Numerous*. This remarkable beginning renders numerousness both as trope and compositional method. In this introduction alone, there are two uncited quotations which Davidson's endnotes locate for us:

> 1. Quoted from Robert Brumbaug's *Plato for the Modern Age*: "And to see them is to know ourselves," which also echoes the epigram in Oppen's *The Materials* in turn quoted from Jacques Maritain's "We awake in the same moment to ourselves and to things"

2. "You remember that old town..." quoted from Mary Oppen speaking about the poetry of Yves Bonnefoy.

Yet I think that neither collage, citational poetics, nor intertextuality can contain Oppen's elaborate inclusion of texts. Perhaps something closer to conversations, to friendships, and to community as these enable composition and thought, can.

The "crisis of being numerous," Michael Davidson writes in his endnotes to *The New Collected Poems*, "haunts all of Oppen's work." "But on a more personal level," Davidson continues "Oppen [signals] the value of friends and family whose comments from letters and conversations have sustained him and which are interspersed throughout the book."

7

Obsessed, bewildered

By the shipwreck
Of the singular

We have chosen the meaning
Of being numerous.

Reading Davidson's endnotes to the Oppen collection, I note that the poet Rachel Blau Duplessis had suggested in a letter to Oppen that he "drop the entire section 7." I tell A this, knowing that we share the same intense fascination for the clarity and courage of that section. "I don't agree really," Oppen responds to Blau Duplessis' suggestion. "I need that,"

Oppen continues, "and need it as flat as it is to establish that half of the burden of the poem which is hardest to establish—the concepts evolved from the fact of being numerous, without which we are marooned, shipwrecked—it is in fact unthinkable without them."

I think that the "meaning of being numerous" which Oppen writes "we have chosen" imagines the individual not only as the individual persists in the grand machines of modernity—of nation, of capital—but also and more significantly the desirous person whose personal desires complicate desire as it becomes shared in the numerousness of loves and friendships, of mass societies and political action.

> We are pressed, pressed on each other

Again, Oppen. And while what he had in mind in 1968 were quite different from now: an altogether different nation, a very different war... I find him and his poetry today, rather persistently, and altogether painfully apt:

18

> It is the air of atrocity,
> An event as ordinary
>
> As a President.
>
> A plume of smoke, visible at a distance
> In which people burn.

09.07.2018

The day always starts at its appointed time. Across multiple time zones. The bank opens at 9 A.M. signaling the start of the market. A day takes shape. In figuring out which day to begin with, which note among these series of notes marked by days I should consider as a beginning, I end up choosing a day that thinks about silence.

In a dream, more white noise, yet present only pictorially, the dream still lacking sound. And somehow, the same notion occurred to us independently, despite the multiple time zones between us, in the meanwhile of the dream. The very nature of beginning, says Arendt, carries in itself an element of complete arbitrariness. She was talking of action, and freedom, and we.

Arendt locates, in the concept of freedom, a possible space for the synthesis of action and thought, a space where action is no longer linked to thought via a causal chain of events, or where thought no longer takes an opposite and less valuable position in relation to action. Where Marx writes that "the philosophers have only interpreted the world... the point however is to change it," Arendt does not read a challenge to philosophy per se, but only to the inconsequentiality of a philosophy as practiced by its professional thinkers—philosophers "resigned to do no more than find a place for themselves in the world, instead of changing the world and making it 'philosophical.'"

"The consequence that Marx drew from Hegel," she writes further, "was that action contrary to the philosophical tradition was so far from being the opposite of thought, that it was its true, namely, real vehicle."

It is through Arendt that action and thought seem to find their appropriate synthesis in the concept of freedom; freedom's meaning oscillates between the I-can and the I-will. The I-will which belongs to the faculty of thinking, and hence requires a self to withdraw itself towards the space of the I, so that it may think; and the I-can which belongs to the domain of action, and hence necessitates the formation of a we. *We is a precondition of action*. It is only when individual selves recognize that they are part of a community, a "human plurality," a "faceless *They*," writes Arendt, that individuals are capable of action.

I want to think that the beginning Arendt writes about, "with its necessary element of complete arbitrariness," is no typical beginning. It is a real beginning—separate from the ceaseless starts that follow the stops in the dailiness of our days—closer, perhaps, to Badiou's notion of the event—material only when we as a *we* come to recognize and act by it.

By selecting a note to begin these series of notes, I inevitably forego particular thoughts, jotted down in earlier days, a number of which I hold dear. I wish to recollect one here, specific to the dream:

Of the dream, Marx writes that the "reform of the consciousness" will come when "people will see that the world has long possessed the dream of a thing—and that it only needs to possess the consciousness of this thing in order to really possess it."

Do you remember what you were thinking? In that dream, of soundless white noise, of multiple time zones, I noticed somehow that the same notions occurred to us independently.

01.06.2019

"We *attend* to each other," says the poet Norma Cole. We *attend*, that is, we go to a place where there is an occasion, and by attending to each other we find in another: this place, an occasion. As poets, it is possible to find this place in language, this occasion in the poem. This attending attention, this tending, is vital, all the more critical, if we are ever to imagine communities formed out of writing and art.

    Benedict Anderson reminds us that the imagined political community of our nation is rooted in language. Although the "emotional legitimacy" that we give our sense of nation has a lot to do with the fact that we share and speak the same language, this same sense of nation, our national consciousness, as Anderson points out, is borne out of many negotiations in the politics of language: between the language of the masses and the official language of the court, in the assembly of multiple and varied idiolects into fewer and more manageable print-languages as necessitated by the evolution of print-capitalism, and in the consequent proliferation of official languages through the educational system. Facets of the idea of nation—on the one hand the official nationalism and myths espoused by markets and states, and on the other the ongoing ideal where we continue to figure out what we mean by *we, the people*, and maintain that collective action allows us to assert our very human values against market and state interests—are what we contend with as we continue with each day. "Politics," Badiou writes, "is enthusiasm with a collective; with love, two people. So love is the minimal form of communism."

R.d.B.

In the wake of the Cuban Missile Crisis in 1961, Oppen wrote "Time of the Missile." I read this poem today, exasperated with how states, how governments acting as machineries of the ruling class, feign their machinations as a sense—however deranged—of nation. The powerful in the guise of nation imperils our very ideals through its myths, and can readily violate our lives and the people we hold most dear.

> I remember a square of New York's Hudson River glinting between
>
> Warehouses.
> Difficult to approach the water below the pier
> Swirling, covered with oil the ship at the pier
> A steel wall: tons in the water,
>
> Width.
> The hand for holding,
> Legs for walking,
> The eye sees! It floods in on us from here to Jersey tangled in the grey bright air!
>
> *Become the realm of nations.*
>
> *My love, my love,*
> *We are endangered*
> *Totally at last. Look*
> *Anywhere to the sight's limit: space*
> *Which is viviparous:*

Place of the mind
And eye. Which can destroy us,
Re-arrange itself, assert
Its own stone chain reaction.

("Time of the Missile" by George Oppen)

R.d.B.

02.12.2019

Someone asked me today, *why do you write poems?*

Was it Foucault who said that action is the intensification of thought? Along this line then, action is not linked to thought as effect is to cause, but rather through a furthering. Elements of thought carried through—carried out— the ethical dimension—as one takes a choice and then another—the gradients by which one proceeds.

Thinking, as a consequence, becomes a furthering of the poem, of poiesis; to find a form, and let thinking traverse the form, describe it, locate its possibilities. A decision point, several decision points—necessary silences—take shape between actions and thoughts. Silence is necessary to the poem, preconditioning thought. We require this silence each time we approach a form, each time we further it, to be able sustain a form in its inexhaustibility.

———

(draft—translation—from Allan Popa's *Modus Operandi*)

1

And we arrive
at a time
when the wrong hand
holds the implements
for work.

Drill, pipe wrench,
acetylene torch, hammer...
What these pulverize
in perforating the wall
is what made them
so as to rebuild
the revered.
We live in
towering ruins,
nothing more can be ascertained.

———

Stéphane Mallarmé shuffles the leaves of his book, *Le Livre*. Today the page which reads "time" "ashes" "the book suppresses" comes before the page where "a crime sewer" "And sorrows" "street". He pauses "towards the relation/ of 8 printed pages" then shuffles the pages again. *The Book* is the "musicality of everything."

"[H]ere moving ahead, there remembering, in the future, in the past, under a false appearance of the present."

At the end of his life, Étienne Mallarmé remembers his unfinished poem. "Destroy it," he says, "it would have been beautiful."

How does one move from the individual towards the collective, from the collective towards an infinite hopefulness?

Our hope requires a solid, material base for its existence, "the crude and material things," Benjamin writes, "without which no refined and spiritual things could exist."

"Nevertheless," he continues:

> [I]t is not in the form of spoils which fall to the victor that [refined and spiritual things] make their presence felt in the class struggle. They manifest themselves in this struggle as courage humor, cunning and fortitude. They have retroactive force and will constantly call into question every victory, past and present of the rulers. As flowers turn toward the sun, by dint of a secret heliotropism, the past strives to turn toward the sun which is rising in the sky of history.

(Oct 2017 – Feb 2019)

BETWEEN THE MAKING OF THIS MOVE AND THIS MOVE

Then left to the quiet of gesture. The shoulders see to it that the arms see to it that the hands. The hands, the fingers. The fingers time, space, then intensity.

"And I don't know whether I can go back again to abstraction," says Trisha Brown after working on Claudio Monteverdi's *L'Orfeo*.

The Monteverdi, whose *chorus of spirits* makes Trisha pace around her studio, asking herself "what is a spirit, what is a spirit," makes her find a vocabulary of movement without

bone structure, that is smoke, intensity

draws forward the head
where the body, while, where the distance
between gesture and movement is a note

or a fullness of presence.

And the distance between gesture and writing is the sign as a sign for itself.

R.d.B.

Dear Jean, we are
lost in the repetition, a color,
or a phrase of movement

recalls to us Écriture Rose by Simon Hantaï —

which begins green,
begins black. Hegel: *In making its
inorganic nature organic
to himself*

and taking possession of it for himself. Looked at, however,

Ends in black. Maintains the missing.
And the quiet is the fold.

Where what is accomplished in writing
is the color rose.

It is after parting ways with surrealism that Simon Hantaï begins his work with folds, begins the search for "an unremarkable painting."

"The underpinning of my work is to create an architecture that is solid," says Trisha Brown "so the audience will know what the changes are."

In working with Bach's *The Musical Offering*, Trisha returns to the question "What is a theme?" takes a walk thinking "what is a theme, what is a theme."

It is fifteen years after withdrawing from the art scene that Simon begins work on *Travaux de lecture* as requested by his friend Jean-Luc

copying, re-copying, copying, re-copying Jean-Luc's and Jacques'

until an unreadable manuscript results on the stiffened and crumpled batiste.

Mailed to Jean-Luc as a gift in March 2000.

Word is where the work turns
is read as color is relation.

So the work
in the economy of the gift must be held in relation
may be word.

Silence whose rigor is a kind of sensuality
and whose sensuality is a line

Asked to put our arms around the work

The section of Trisha Brown's *Set and Reset* where she dances with Eva Karczag and her gestural movements are mirrored by Eva's balletic motion.

The shadow of the musculature on their backs
from the lighting design
of Robert Rauschenberg.

R.d.B.

Dear Jean, we are chosen for how we sound. Dance means deixis as a fullness in the present.

Before Simon Hantaï's silence, some shorter silences, and several pliage works: *Etudes et blancs, Tabula* —

which Simon destroys, buries, and after his return from silence, unearths, and makes into new work which he calls *Leftovers*.

There is a photograph of Trisha Brown performing *Watermotor* (shot by Babette Mangolte) where she seems to be moving simultaneously to her left and to her right.

"My father died in between the making of this move and this move," Trisha finds herself saying in a performance of *Accumulation with Talking Plus Watermotor*.

In lieu of a biography, Simon Hantaï includes in the catalogue of his 1976 retrospective a photograph of a large unfolded painting, and a grainy, black and white picture of his mother wearing a dark, creased, gridded tablier.

"And I don't know whether I can go back to abstraction again," Trisha Brown says after working on *L'Orfeo*.

THE IMAGE AS A KNOWLEDGE OF SPACE
(WRITTEN FOR MARC GABA'S PROPERTY OF SPACE)

This is a book of images, of the image as space, of the image as a production of space, of the distance between image and text. An image is not an object. Objects contain matter; an image contains. It is a book about what an image can contain, about what a text can contain, how a work can conflate image and text, then how in such conflation relations are severed. I propose that it says the image has a knowledge of space. The image is an agent of epistemology. What knowledge does it contain? As an agent, it acquires and creates. It knows of the nature and availability of space. It creates them. The book starts with a premise. *Premise (Duchamp).* Then *Premise (Question of Trespass).* Remember that a premise is a proposition. And that the premises is a place. Space is delimited in the declaration of place. It is a double operation: an image produces knowledge of the evening, the silhouette of a water tank, two burlap garbage bags, a toilet, a no-parking sign; then the no-parking sign carves out a separate space within the space. A proper space. Inappropriable. Then *Premise (Guest).* Now we have three premises, enough to form an argumentative structure. We understand that these are not pictures of a landscape. "The landscape," Jean-Luc Nancy writes, "is the contrary of a ground." "In it must be entirely surface," and surface alone "throughout." Instead we have something like receding picture frames—the ground of evening, the figure of a place (the silhouette of a water tank, a makeshift eatery, corrugated roof for a wall), and the becoming of a figure, the fuzzy delimitations of no-parking spaces. So the space in the image is no longer representational space. No longer just figure and ground. But a virtual space, where we see the taking place of space.

Then a section where we are shown closer shots of the no-parking signs. *Sign (sculpture)*—where the text is almost effaced. *Sign (leap)*—where the sign is broken. In *Sign (Alphabet Accordion)*, the sign is almost illegible. In *Sign (Meadow)*, it is draped in leaf-shadows. Here, the no-parking space that is taking place (that took place in the Premises) is larger than the frame of the image. Becoming is outside the border. What we have is the sign broken, estranged, a rupture in the signifying chain, an estrangement in the signifying relations. "Painting silences language," Agamben says "returning the thing to itself, to its namelessness." In *Middle Distance*, the signs waver in their namelessness in the spaces between figure and ground.

But the no-parking sign, revealed in its not-referring to the no-parking space, is a potentially genial trace. What it reveals, presents, creates, borrowing again from Agamben, is the thing in its "pure sayability." Such that an image, as space, has knowledge of the pure sayability of objects:

Marc Gaba, *Page from Where We Stand*, 2016, oil on canvas, 24 x 30 in.

Dear Marc,

I want to use the form of the letter in engaging with the works found in the exhibit, and the form of essay when discussing the images in the book. By placing these formal restrictions, I hope to enact something of a shift in approach (a difference in attitudes, which I feel is imperative, between engaging with an exhibit, and essaying a response to a book), and also to enact a formal border between the site of the exhibit and the site of the book, when, as you say the "images move across the two sites."

When you directed my attention to the impasto stripes you added above the "AN" in the "MANILA" of this painting, and then wrote of your recent interest in exploring how abstraction incorporates content, I was reminded of Rosalind Krauss's essay on the Grid where she talks about how the grid, "by its very abstraction, conveyed one of the basic laws of knowledge—the separation of the perceptual screen from that of the 'real' world." I think that through Krauss, it becomes apparent that what abstraction contains, the content it incorporates, is not knowledge, but something like the knowledge of knowledge.

And isn't that (*The Knowledge of Knowledge*) the title of one of your shows which had the *Surface Variation* series a couple of years back?

Marc Gaba, Love (They, Utrillo, Alteration Make), 2016, oil and inkjet print on canvas, 47 x 60 in.

When you mentioned Maurice Utrillo, his paintings which reveal what you described as the clarity of space between the shut buildings of early 20th century Paris, I thought about

Utrillo's skies which I felt is central to his paintings. As if all the impressionist buildings, streets and trees were made to frame the clarity of his skies.

By containing in this one work a number of gestures—impasto lines, geometric planes, unpainted photograph—the image becomes a site of contested epistemologies. The abstract elements attempt to organize knowledge of a space, while the unpainted space (if one were to think of the photograph as a limit of naturalistic representation) attempts to present it, despite the agency engulfing its organization.

———

Marc Gaba, Apologia for Mondrian, 2016, oil and inkjet print on canvas, 12 x 16 in.

In appropriating Mondrian's *Composition with Yellow Lines*, and keeping only the yellow, where you deftly replaced (and also pointed out) that the blanc (white) is replaced with a blank, and is also a noir (both the color black, and the noir of the photograph), I am fascinated with how through an entanglement among words and an actual compositional transformation, color becomes space. Mondrian, of course, figured a lot in the Krauss essay. But there is also in her essay a commentary on the paintings of Seurat, Signac, Cross, and Luce, who while applying in their paintings the lessons of physiological optics, were in fact making more abstract art—the critic Felix Feneon observing that "science began to yield its opposite, which is symbolism."

In the final section, titled *Space*, the space produced by the no-parking sign finds itself in conflict with the space seemingly produced by other elements in the image: the streetlamp in *Prayer*, the broken sidewalk in *Altruism*, the private space in *Visible Life*. In the final image, we are presented with an empty sign, which we can take as a pun on the empty signifier, the floating signifier, which in our experience of this book has moved along a floating chain of signifiers: political, epistemological, phenomenological and ontological.

A PORTRAITURE
(WRITTEN FOR ALLAN BALISI'S *THE SMALLEST CONVENIENCE*)

Benjamin recounts in his essay "A Short History of Photography," that "the real victim of photography was not landscape painting, but the miniature portrait." Such was photography's initial effect on portraiture, that, in a little over ten years after the first photograph was taken, "most of the innumerable miniature painters [...] had already become professional photographers."

It has been almost 90 years since Benjamin's essay and in the intervening years, the hand that photographic techniques (and later filmic techniques) have had on the expansion of the field of painting, is inarguable. But the immediate, and obvious consequence of photography was that, instead of being an affront to painting, it only added more objects to the objects of the world: a photograph became another thing to be painted. At its nascent stage, the photograph's relationship to painting was that of a "technical adjunct."

Benjamin gives account of Maurice Utrillo, who in 1910, "painted his fascinating views of Paris not from life, but from picture postcards," and of David Octavius Hill, who painted frescoes from a series of portrait photographs that he himself took, and who later on would become more widely known for his stash of photographic aids than for his paintings. From these preliminary examples, painting's interest in photography will take on countless generative turns along with the proliferation of modes and variants of the contemporary photograph: the film still, the screen capture, pictures on social media platforms, etc.

In the 1960s, when Clement Greenberg asserted abstraction's role as the primary mode of modernist painting, Francis Bacon painted from photographs and film images, and in effect generated other possibilities for the figurative in painting:

Interview 1, 1966

DAVID SYLVESTER: It's interesting that the photographic image you've worked from most of all isn't a scientific or a journalistic one but a very deliberate and famous work of art – the still of the scream from Potemkin.

FRANCIS BACON: It was a film I saw almost before I started to paint, and it deeply impressed me – I mean the whole film as well as the Odessa Steps sequence and this shot. I did hope at one time to make – it hasn't got any special significance – I did hope one day to make the best painting of the human cry. I was not able to do it and it's much better in the Eisenstein and there it is. I think probably the best human cry in painting was made by Poussin...

―――

Allan Balisi operates in painting's filmic and photographic spaces. He is aware of the questions that image making, replicating, and archiving technologies pose to the significance of contemporary painting practice, and he contends with these questions by making them the necessary conditions for his works. His relationship to filmic and photographic techniques has spanned numerous shows and publications. In his show titled *In Between Open Fields* (Blanc Gallery, 2015) we find a series of paintings of images sourced from screen captures of low resolution, drive-in movies; in *People I Don't Know, and Places I've Never Been* (Blanc Gallery, 2016), ink drawings of vintage photographs he bought from a thrift shop; and pronouncedly, in his picture book *Everyone Exists Forever* (Self-published, 2016), with its subtitle *Thirty Three Film Endings/ Thirty Three Drawings*, pages of drawings of the closing scenes of various films.

While in most of Ballisi's shows and books, the photograph takes on the role of source image (at times cited, though more often not), a slightly different but nonetheless engaging dynamic between painting and photography is at work in his minimally designed book *Painting Study* (Saturnino Basilia, 2015). In *Painting Study*, Balisi presents us with pages of photos of an unnamed man "who from his initial static, standing pose," he says "was then given the instruction to fall." Yet we see that even in this photography work, the consistently muted color tonality, which we find in most of his paintings, persists:

Image from Painting Study, Allan Balisi, 2015

Balisi takes more than source images from film. His process involves sifting through a voluminous amount of pictorial material, physical (second hand books, found photos, etc.) and virtual (streamed movies, online videos, etc.), zooming into and/or cropping out details from these images, then replicating them in tonally consistent painterly conditions. His selection procedure bears, in a number of aspects, similarities to the work of film editing, or more specifically to the composition of filmic montage.

But what value can the decontextualized image still have given our contemporary realities—realities that include the overabundance of images and the deliberate repurposing of these images for disinformation? Perhaps we can look to the dynamic of image and gesture, through possibilities offered by Agamben when he thinks of this dynamic via the cinematic image.

In Agamben, gesture is neither a means to an end, nor the *means* as an end in itself. Although he locates gesture in the sphere of action, he describes it as the mode of action where "nothing is produced or acted [but rather, where] *something is* [...] endured or supported." Gesture then is a form of pure potential, a sheer condition for the possibility of choice, and therefore the possibility of an ethics. For Agamben, the value of gesture is that, there is, through it the immanent reminder that "there is no essence, no historical or spiritual vocation, no biological destiny that humans must enact or realize."

Through gesture "something like an ethics can exist, because it is clear that if humans were or had to be this or that substance, this or that destiny, [then] no ethics would be possible—there would only be tasks to be done." Agamben finds in cinema, a paramount method for the recording of gestures. By emphasizing that a film, in a nod to Gilles Delueze, is composed not merely of sequences of static images, but rather by "image-movements" themselves, he underscores the capacity of the cinematic image to exhibit "pure mediality," to make "a means visible as such."

The images in Allan Balisi's *The Smallest Convenience* are drawn from medical books, hospital archives, first aid brochures, instructional medical videos, and similar such sources. "I am still interested in narrative, but with more interest in the idea that the viewers will make what they will of the images rather than attempt to reconstruct the original narratives from them," Balisi speaks of a plausible effect of his work. His interest then is not in narrative per se, but in the gestural potential of the image to open up narrative, or, to push the idea further and perhaps more variously, his engagement lies in the images' capacity to merely open *something* up.

His works in *The Smallest Convenience* are hardly bound by narrative, but are tied rather, and to a greater degree by a particular typology: bandages, prostheses, gauze, the injured figure given medical attention, the medical worker in the act of preparing various medical implements. Rendering these images in the consistent tonality that pervades his works, our attention is drawn away from the pictures' connotative implications, and towards the movement of images from one denotative system to another, that is, from the denotative system of medical instruction, to a signature painterly rendering of particular types. In *The Smallest Convenience*, the type in focus is that of the figure of and around the damaged body.

The Smallest Convenience is an investigation of gestures and gesturality. In *Viridian State of Grace*, a woman is absorbed in what seems like the preparation of bandage from gauze; someone is attending to an injured knee in *According to Ovid's Description of Feathered Cloaks*; a hand is laying down what is likely a model for prosthetic arms in *To Identify as Imitating*. Gesturality is manifest not only in Balisi's figures that are caught mid-action, but even in his method of painting as well.

Of recent changes in his painting approach, he says: "I used to work by applying layers of paint, then scraping the layers off to achieve the subdued color of my paintings, but in my more recent works, I produce the subdued effect by a layer- by-layer application of thin, diluted paint."

There is a marked expressiveness of details in Balisi's paintings. We notice, for instance, the attention that he gives to his figures' heads of hair, how detailed the locks and waves of hair are, for examples, in *Mending Figure* and *Pursuing the Sight*, or how the expressive creases of hair of the woman-figure are echoed in the green folds of dress in *Viridian State of Grace*.

It is also notable that Balisi's figures rarely fully expose their faces—a motif that persists in his shows and publications. In certain extremes, Balisi's figures face away from the viewer, exposing only their characteristic heads of hair. Often, his figures attend to tasks that seemingly require their absolute focus, giving them no chance to turn towards what could-have-been the depictions of their faces.

Balisi comments on portraiture by excluding the face, by locating expressiveness in gestures and in creases, by giving extraneous details the expressive qualities we would normally find in the face. In a number of instances, the figures have their heads slightly bowed down, or turned to an edgewise angle. This particular motif is one we find in *Triumph in Disguise* where we catch the slight profile of a man wearing a pair of glasses that are tenuously held by gauze. Yet the man's face seems to communicate nothing beyond the adhesive bandages covering up his bruises and wounds. In what may be a playful turn, we find that there is much more attention given to the details of the man's varicolored, camouflage shirt. The closest to standard portraiture that Balisi gets to in *The Smallest Convenience* is with the painting that shares the show's title: *The Smallest Convenience (Beautiful, Noble, Necessary)*. Here we have a man slightly looking edgewise, but this time remarkably with his eyes fully exposed, his face given further expression by his well-formed nose and lips. His face is bathed in reddish light, strands of his hair slightly cover the top of his right ear. In the subdued red light of overexposure, we find patches of green pigment in the skin of his forehead, chin, and cheeks. But with a closer inspection of his cheek, there is a wound dressing—an adhesive bandage likely covering a scratch or a bruise—repeating the show's theme. Perhaps, and somewhat playfully, Balisi reminds us that with the exponential proliferation of the image, portraiture more and more becomes another system of typology.

Allan Balisi, Smallest Convenience (Beautiful, Noble, Necessary), 2018, oil on canvas, 18 x 22 in.

A HOUSE COLLAGED WITH PITCH CLASS SPACE

Daylight glosses the living room floors of M. and Mme. Leiseville at 27-29 rue Beaubourg.

Daylight at a doorless threshold, from several iterations of Les Halles, from the construction site of the Centre Pompidou.

Daylight at the rubble-edges of Gordon Matta-Clark's *Conical Intersect*.

Then daylight at the apex, collapses, of a person's cone of vision.

We expect the high-pitched ring that accompanies suddenly something bright

instead of silence annexed to shimmer, interior glow, found sounds, an audience pointing to the sun, and a critique of modern housing.

Cones of vision and funnels of hearing emanate from an audience, transform the light-holes into points of articulation.

Construction sounds enter our gardens.

Passersby with their wobbly cones and funnels escape analysis.

R.d.B.

The "particular agony" that Toru Takemitsu finds "in the sound of the door someone closed" is our hearing in place of analysis.

We are when our geometric imagination meets social space, a schematic diagram of a house collaged with pitch class space.

The semi-circular incisions across floors, ceilings, and walls involve chisels, saws, hammers, and an extraordinary amount of sound.

"Gardens are constructions of space," says Takemitsu, "so really what I do is compose gardens with music."

Gardens with construction sounds strain toward the present.

Perhaps, a light-split wall is how composition intersects construction as the immaterial spatially arranging,

or a movement where the phrase sustained by an oboe continues to the shō.

The moments after his dream, where Toru begins to compose *A Flock Descends into a Pentagonal Garden*.

A shape that is a modulation, and not a modularity.

A morning, when we are, where construction is composition.

The shape that sound acquires from trusses, rubble, incision, this pastoral's dream content, our found ways of being, Dear Jean, the varied surfaces of our listenings, "a lyrical cutting through"

suffused with light, where dream and labor intersect.

WORKS CITED

Agamben, Giorgio. "Image and Silence." Translated by Leland Durantaye. *Diacritics* 40, no. 2 (2012).
———. *Infancy and History: The Destruction of Experience*. Translated by Liz Heron. New York: Verso Books, 1993.
———. *Means Without End*. Translated by Cesare Casarino and Vincenzo Binetti. Minneapolis: University of Minnesota Press, 2000.
———. *The Coming Community*. Translated by Michael Hardt. Minneapolis: University of Minnesota Press, 1993.
———. *The End of the Poem*. Translated by Daniel Heller-Roazen. Stanford, CA: Stanford University Press, 1996.
Anderson, Benedict. *Imagined Communities*. London: Verso, 2006.
Arendt, Hannah. *The Life of the Mind*. Edited by Mary McCarthy. Orlando, FL: Harcourt, 1978.
———. *Thinking Without a Bannister: Essays in Understanding, 1953-1975*. Edited by Jerome Kohn. New York: Schocken Books, 2018.
Badiou, Alain. *Being and Event*. Translated by Oliver Feltham. New York: Continuum, 2007.
———. "Fifteen Theses on Contemporary Art." *Lacan.com*, 2004. http://www.lacan.com/frameXXIII7.htm.
———. *Handbook of Inaesthetics*. Translated by Rodrigo Toscano. Stanford, CA: Stanford University Press, 2005.
———. *Number and Numbers*. Translated by Robin Mackay. Cambridge, UK: Polity, 2008.
———. "On the Truth-Process Followed by Interventions of S. Zizek and G. Agamben." *Lacan.com*, 2002. http://www.lacan.com/badeurope.htm.

———. "The Subject of Art." Lacan.com, 2005. http://www.lacan.com/symptom6_articles/badiou.html.
Benjamin, Walter. "A Short History of Photography." Translated by Stanley Mitchell. *Screen* 13, no. 1 (March 1972): 5-26.
———. *Illuminations: Essays and Reflections*. Edited by Hannah Arendt. New York: Schocken Books, 2007.
Berssenbrugge, Mei-mei. *Four Year Old Girl*. Berkeley, CA: Kelsey St. Press, 1998.
———. *I Love Artists: New and Selected Poems*. Berkeley, CA: University of California Press, 2006.
Blanchot, Maurice. *Friendship*. Translated by Elizabeth Rottenberg. Stanford, CA: Stanford University Press, 1997.
Celan, Paul. *Der Meridian und Andere Prosa*. Baden-Baden: Suhrkamp Verlag, 1988.
———. *Collected Prose*. Translated by Rosmarie Waldrop. Riverdale-on-Hudson, NY: The Sheep Meadow Press, 1986.
———. *Selected Poems and Prose*. Translated by John Felstiner. New York: W.W. Norton, 2001.
———. *Snow Part*. Translated by Ian Fairley. New York: Sheep Meadow Press, 2007.
Christensen, Inger. *Alphabet*. Translated by Susanna Nied. New York: New Directions, 2001.
Davenport, Guy. *Twelve Stories*. Berkeley, CA: Counterpoint, 1997.
DeLanda, Manuel. *Intensive Science and Virtual Philosophy*. New York: Bloomsbury, 2013.
Deleuze, Gilles, and Félix Guattari. *A Thousand Plateaus*. Translated by Brian Massumi. New York: Continuum, 1988.
Deleuze, Gilles, and Claire Parnet. *Dialogues*. Translated by Hugh Tomlinson and Barbara Habberjam. New York: Columbia University Press, 1987.
Dickinson, Emily. *The Complete Poems of Emily Dickinson*. Edited by Thomas Johnson. Boston: Little, Brown and Company, 1960.
Dolar, Mladen. *A Voice and Nothing More*. Cambridge, MA: MIT Press, 2006.

Works Cited

Gelley, Alexander. *Benjamin's Passages: Dreaming, Awakening.* New York: Fordham University Press, 2014.

Guest, Barbara. *Collected Poems of Barbara Guest.* Edited by Hadley Guest. Middletown, CT: Wesleyan University Press, 2008.

Heidegger, Martin. *Being and Time.* Translated by John Macquarrie and Edward Robinson. New York: Harper & Row, 1962.

Hejinian, Lyn. *The Book of a Thousand Eyes.* Richmond, CA: Omnidawn Publishing, 2012.

———. *The Language of Inquiry.* Berkeley: University of California Press, 2000.

Howe, Fanny. *Selected Poems.* Berkeley: University of California Press, 2000.

Howe, Susan. *That This.* New York: New Directions, 2010.

Krauss, Rosalind. "Grids." *October* 9 (Summer 1979): 50–64.

Mackey, Nathaniel. *Splay Anthem.* New York: New Directions, 2006.

Mallarmé, Stéphane. *Divagations.* Translated by Barbara Johnson. Cambridge, MA: Harvard University Press, 2009.

———. "Excerpt from Le Livre." In *Poems for the Millennium*, edited by Jerome Rothenberg and Pierre Joris. Berkeley: University of California Press, 1995.

———. *Selected Poetry and Prose.* Translated by Mary Ann Caws. New York: New Directions, 1982.

Matta-Clark, Gordon. *Conical Intersect.* 1975. Photograph. Artnet. Accessed December 27, 2011.

Nancy, Jean-Luc. *Listening.* Translated by Charlotte Mandell. Bronx, NY: Fordham University Press, 2007.

———. *The Ground of the Image.* Translated by Jeff Fort. New York: Fordham University Press, 2005.

Oppen, George. *New Collected Poems.* Edited by Michael Davidson. New York: New Directions, 2002.

Popa, Allan. *Modus Operandi.* Katipunan: Talaantala, 2017.

Robertson, Lisa. *Nilling.* Toronto: BookThug, 2012.

Roubaud, Jacques. *The Great Fire of London: Story with Interpolations and Bifurcations.* Translated by Dominic Di Bernardi. Normal, IL: Dalkey Archive Press, 1991.

Works Cited

Shklovsky, Viktor. "Art as Technique." In *Russian Formalist Criticism: Four Essays*, 2nd ed., edited by Lee T. Lemon and Marion J. Reis. Lincoln: University of Nebraska Press, 2012.

Spicer, Jack. *My Vocabulary Did This to Me: The Collected Poetry of Jack Spicer*. Edited by Peter Gizzi and Kevin Killian. Middletown, CT: Wesleyan University Press, 2008.

Sylvester, David. *Interviews with Francis Bacon*. London: Thames & Hudson, 2016.

Takemitsu, Toru. *Confronting Silence: Selected Writings*. Edited by Yoshiko Kakudo and Glenn Glasow. Lanham, MD: Scarecrow Press, 1995.

Waldrop, Keith. *Transcendental Studies*. Oakland, CA: University of California Press, 2009.

Weil, Simone. *Gravity and Grace*. Translated by Emma Crawford and Mario von der Ruhr. New York: Routledge, 2002.

Wieners, John. *The Journal of John Wieners Is to Be Called 707 Scott Street for Billie Holiday, 1959*. Los Angeles: Sun and Moon Press, 1996.

Williams, William Carlos. *Selected Poems*. Edited by Charles Tomlinson. New York: New Directions, 1985.

Wyeth, Andrew. *Wind from the Sea*. 1948. Private collection. Accessed December 27, 2011.

"Enter the Garden: Toru Takemitsu." BBC. 2008. Accessed May 14, 2012.

Eternity and a Day. Directed by Theo Angelopoulos. Paris: Paradis Films, 1998.

"John Zorn Documentary." YouTube video, 2008. Accessed May 14, 2012.

The Face of Another. Directed by Hiroshi Teshigahara. The Criterion Collection, 2007. DVD.

"Property of Space." Artery Art Space, Cubao, Quezon City. June 18–July 9, 2016.

"The Smallest Convenience." Blanc Gallery, Katipunan, Quezon City. December 8, 2018–January 5, 2019.

"Where or When." Silverlens. Accessed December 8, 2013.

ACKNOWLEDGMENTS

Versions of the essays and poems here were published in *as well, in our estrangement* (Aklat Ulagad, 2022) and *facture* (Broken Sleep Books, 2024). I am thankful to the editors and teams of Aklat Ulagad, and Broken Sleep Books for their support.

I am also grateful to the editors and staff of various journals where these works first appeared: *Heavy Feather Review, Jacket2, Kritika Kultura, The Operating System, Tomas, The White Review*.

"The Image as a Knowledge of Space" was written for Marc Gaba's show "Property of Space" (Artery Art Space, Cubao, Quezon City, June 18-July 9, 2016).

"Aportraiture" was written for Allan Balisi's show "The Smallest Convenience" (Blanc Gallery, Katipunan, Quezon City, Dec 8, 2018 – Jan 5, 2019

And to friends whose company, conversation, and invitation to write and talk served as prompts for pieces in this book: Mark Cayanan, Vincenz Serrano, Conchitina Cruz, Nanoy Rafael, Ergoe Tinio, Allan Popa, Marc Gaba, and Allan Balisi.

OTHER BUNNY TITLES

1. **Warren Longmire**—*BIRD/DIZ [an erased history of bebop]* (print)

2. **Bill Carty**—*We Sailed on the Lake* (print)

3. **Zoe Tuck**—*Bedroom Vowel* (print)

4. **Michael Wheaton**—*Home Movies* (print)

5. **Jennifer Quartararo**—*An Aribtrary Formation of Unspecified Value* (print)

6. **Matthew Broaddus**—*Deeper the Tropics* (print)

7. **Katie Naughton**—*Debt Ritual* (print)

8. **Marina Blitshteyn**—*Landguage/Mirror Me* (print)

Inspired by the work of the multitudinous artist Ray Johnson, BUNNY is an imprint of Fonograf Editions. Publishing a wide variety of works, BUNNY is looking towards the future while thinking about the past.

www.ingramcontent.com/pod-product-compliance
Lightning Source LLC
LaVergne TN
LVHW090041080526
838202LV00046B/3914